Praise for *Your Network Is Your Net Worth*

"Be authentic, follow your passions, nurture relationships, and use technology to improve and accelerate your connections. This is a great read with insightful stories and lots of practical tips. Not to mention that Porter has executed this, not just talked about it."

—Gary Vaynerchuk, author of *Crush It!* and *The Thank You Economy*; founder VaynerMedia and Winelibrary.tv

"This book could not have come at a better time. Today, when our networks are more valuable than ever before, Porter offers the tools that will help us tap into our connections in a way that effortlessly brings exponential returns to our lives and relationships."

—Randi Zuckerberg, CEO and founder of Zuckerberg Media

"In a time when we all need to learn how to unlock our human potential and make meaningful connections, Porter masterfully articulates the pathways. This is a must-have-read."

—David Mayer de Rothschild, British adventurer/environmentalist and author

"Like a modern-day Dale Carnegie, Porter unpacks the power of connections that will help all of us unleash the full potential of our professional careers and personal lives. This is the book I wish I had at the start of my career!"

—Eric Ryan, cofounder of method

"In a connected society, we are defined by what we say, what we do, and who we know. As in the real world, social capital is now the measure of one's standing in these digital communities. Porter Gale explains how each of us can more productively contribute to this social economy."

—Brian Solis, digital analyst, sociologist and best-selling author

"Look at the names on and in this book. Porter's title isn't just a cute quip; she's built a priceless collection of friends, colleagues and contacts using it as a mantra, and so can you."

—Ryan Holiday, director of marketing, American Apparel

"Porter's book defines one of the most important and critical missing components of the digital age. That no matter how advanced or powerful or connected our digital equipment is, at the end of the day we are human, and that in itself is the most useful tool we have to create the world we want to live in."

—Nick Graham, founder of Joe Boxer

"Porter's a connector. In fact she's introduced me to more people than I can count. Her book includes the recipe and the secret sauce for networking."

—Michael Mina, celebrity chef and owner of eighteen restaurants

"Finally, someone has offered real, practical advice on how to grow and flourish as a person amongst all the social technology that surrounds us. *Your Network Is Your Net Worth* is a must-have guide to success in today's connected world."

—Courtney Buechert, CEO of Eleven, Inc.

"They say it's who you know, not what you know. While this is not entirely true, your network is in fact a crucial tool in advancing toward your own personal goal line. Porter's advice is built on real-life success. Your network *is* your net worth."

—Jason Felts, CEO of Virgin Produced

"Wonder how to 'be' in social media? First you have to know who you are. Candid yet caring, Porter Gale unlocks the secret of social media success by sharing a core truth: It's what you give to the experience that determines what you get. With Porter's counsel, you'll learn how helping others—people, issues, products—in whom *you* truly believe will develop a rock-solid foundation for your own social media brand."

—Lisa Stone, cofounder and CEO of BlogHer Inc.

"Want to bring value to the people you connect? With currency, credibility, and unvarnished honesty, Porter creates a brilliant model of networking for a meaningful purpose. Relating stories of personal challenge while driving efforts at some of the world's most valuable brands she derives and shares hard-earned tools that anybody can put to work."

—Jennifer Aaker and Andy Smith,
authors of *The Dragonfly Effect*

"In a noisy and busy world, Porter's book helps you focus on the opportunities that matter and act on them. Her advice comes to life through her own fascinating anecdotes as well as in interviews and stories with the key players of Silicon Valley."

—Bill Clerico, CEO of WePay

"This book is a must-read for anyone who wants to thrive in today's connected culture. Networks are exponential, and networked people are exponentially successful."

—Jon Bond, marketing thought leader and
cofounder of Kirshenbaum Bond Senecal and Partners

"A thoroughly absorbing and enjoyable book that challenges the contemporary conventions of networking, while leaving the reader wanting more. This book makes one thing abundantly clear: Porter Gale is a renaissance woman whose literary vision is as dynamic and impactful as her entrepreneurial track record."

"I've seen Porter rise and network herself from a junior account executive to one of the most well-respected advertising executives in the United States. If you want to know how to connect your way to success, read this book and start increasing your net worth!"

"Porter highlights the significance and value of strategically building your network to improve your personal and professional prosperity."

"This is the first book that addresses the 'me' in social media. Porter is one of America's most successful creative thinkers, and in this generous book full of inspiring stories and easy-to-follow tips and exercises, she teaches us all how to think like marketers and how to build more productive lives filled with purpose, passion, and creativity."

Your Network Is Your Net Worth

Susan -
Thanks for your
support.
Happy connecting.
Best,
Porty Gale

Your Network

Is

Your Net Worth

Unlock the Hidden Power of Connections
for Wealth, Success, and Happiness
in the Digital Age

Porter Gale

Foreword by Guy Kawasaki

ATRIA BOOKS

New York   London   Toronto   Sydney   New Delhi

ATRIA BOOKS

Atria Books
A Division of Simon & Schuster, Inc.
1230 Avenue of the Americas
New York, NY 10020

First Atria Books hardcover edition June 2013

ATRIA BOOKS and colophon are trademarks of Simon & Schuster, Inc.

For information about special discounts for bulk purchases,
please contact Simon & Schuster Special Sales at 1-866-506-1949 or
business@simonandschuster.com.

The Simon & Schuster Speakers Bureau can bring authors to your live event.
For more information or to book an event contact the Simon & Schuster
Speakers Bureau at 1-866-248-3049 or visit our website at
www.simonspeakers.com.

Designed by Ruth Lee-Mui

Manufactured in the United States of America

10   9   8   7   6   5   4   3   2   1

Library of Congress Cataloging-in-Publication Data

Gale, Porter.
Your network is your net worth / by Porter Gale ; foreword by Guy Kawasaki.
— First Atria Books hardcover edition.
p.   cm
Includes bibliographical references and index.
1. Social networks. 2. Online social networks. 3. Social media.
4. Interpersonal relations. 5. Success. I. Title.
HM741.G337 2013
302.30285—dc23   2012049195

ISBN 978-1-4516-8875-7
ISBN 978-1-4516-8878-8 (ebook)

Contents

Part I
Develop a Transformational Attitude

Foreword

Appropriately, I met Porter on Twitter. We initially connected through a project for Virgin America and then I started running into her at book signings, speaking events, conferences, and fundraisers. She once brought a busload of people, in a ride looking like a roving disco, to a benefit for the 49ers Foundation, and my wife and I joined her group. She brought her mom to an event at our house and somewhere along the way we became friends.

With her energy and gift for making meaningful connections, it makes perfect sense that Porter's book is about networking. This book isn't a rehash of stuffy, old-world networking ideas. It's about sharing passions and sensibilities to create authentic, enchanting, and long-lasting connections. Porter's book touches on the ideas that I've embraced in my writing: Be kind. Be passionate. Be enchanting.

Your Network Is Your Net Worth will show you how to establish, grow, and strengthen your connections with others—both online and offline. It is both a primer and a storybook, which will inspire you with amazing stories of well-known business icons and everyday people who have transformed their lives through networking.

In these pages you will learn how to use the best available tools and methods to help you achieve remarkable results. Enjoy!

Guy Kawasaki

Author of *Enchantment* and

former chief evangelist of Apple

Introduction

Chances are that if you are reading this book you are currently in a process of assessment. You may be facing a challenge—a career interruption or transition, a new life stage, or perhaps a financial difficulty—that you are trying to overcome. Or you may be working toward a specific goal in your personal or professional life and need to find the missing link that will take you into the final stretch.

If you are one of the millions who are aspiring to do better— in work, relationships, and financial growth—you have probably found that the process of assessment is a constant companion, and making a change in one area of your life inevitably calls for an evaluation of others. I have gone through this process enough times, during career moves and relationship bumps, to know that in order to make a positive change you need to have a sense of your overall net worth. And by "net worth," I don't mean the status of your financial accounts.

I believe in the power of social capital to improve your productivity, expand your professional options, and raise your overall quality of life. I believe that seeking out and working in collaboration with others who share your interests and values will provide a stronger foundation, enabling you to reach a higher level of success than you would on your own. I believe in the power of connections, not just between people but between passion and productivity, between value and profit, between authenticity and purpose, and ultimately between your heart and your wallet. Therefore, I believe that your "net worth" will be based not on the size of your portfolio but on your ability to define and stay true to your passions and values and that working with other people who share them will allow you to build a strong and enduring interpersonal safety net that will carry you through any financial calamity to greater output and personal fulfillment.

In *Your Network Is Your Net Worth*, I will show you how to unlock the hidden power of connections. And I will show you why your social capital, or your ability to build a network of authentic personal and professional relationships, not your financial capital, is the most important asset in your portfolio. I will show you why your net worth should be measured based on relationships, happiness, productivity, and job satisfaction and not solely in dollars and cents.

I will explain why strengthening and growing your *network* is the fastest way to improve your real net worth. For years, net worth was a quantified number or a collection of assets. In *Your Network Is Your Net Worth*, I will show you why investing in your network is the new model for improving your real net worth.

This kind of worth—wealth as interpersonal creative riches—is at the heart of my approach to networking. Fortunately, the postindustrial, information-age economy that has so profoundly altered the way we build our worth has also provided us with countless new tools to do so. In this book I will show you how I, along with other entrepreneurs and business leaders, have used these tools creatively to build our networks to achieve happiness, success, and true wealth.

In *Your Network Is Your Net Worth*, I will give you clear steps, tools, and ideas to use to build and grow your network. The process of connecting to like-minded people for pleasure and profit, though timeless in concept, has, since the rise of information technology, altered dramatically in methods and potential. The days of mandatory reading of the daily newspapers or bestseller lists to impress someone at a cocktail party, sharing the latest office gossip to bond with a colleague, or controlling your subordinates as you claw your way to the top are past. We've entered a new era where shifting cultural values and improved technology enable us to network in vastly improved, more focused, and more enjoyable ways that are more in tune with our personalities and passions.

The old way to network involved climbing a ladder while pushing others down or to the side for individual benefit. The past was about competition, pursuit of materialism and "keeping up with the Joneses." Networking was all about your position in the game and the number of degrees on your résumé or titles placed after your name. This process worked for some people, to be sure, but not for most. Thankfully, networking has evolved from a transactional game into a transformational process. It's not just about "who you know," it's about "who you are becoming as a person." The new way to network and build your true net worth is about charting your own course, living life based on your passions, and being the best you can be. In today's world, what's important is no longer about power plays but more about what you value and how—and with whom—you want to get there.

Another reason that having a strong network is important is that how we work, along with the role of the employer, has been completely transformed. Globalization, changes in digital technology, and a wavering economy have made tens of millions of corporate positions more contingent and less secure. A 2010

Deloitte survey found that nearly half of all employees say a loss of trust in their employers will cause them to look for a new job when the economy improves. What's more, between 1999 and 2010, the share of workers who said they were satisfied with their job dropped from 59 percent to 25 percent. The reality is that no matter how much you like your job or your company, you can, at any given time, be forced into unemployment.

With few workplace guarantees, it's important to recognize your best path to job security is yourself. The more adaptive, flexible, and agile you are, the more you'll succeed. Look internally, not externally, for happiness and job security. Build your skill sets, improve your network, ask questions, and don't assume that others will take charge of your career.

There is a bright lining to the new model of networking, employment, and globalization. Millions of determined professionals are now creating and fueling a dynamic and innovative new culture of entrepreneurship and virtual teams free from the constraints of the old corporate culture. In *Your Network Is Your Net Worth*, I will share stories that demonstrate how technology has accelerated how we connect and reduced the degree of separation between people. Whether you are excited or discouraged by the bewildering array of social media choices, *Your Network Is Your Net Worth* will illustrate how and why technology and social media can help improve your networking productivity and how you can use them wisely.

When I learned to express my own voice and started using today's tools, I broke through to a new level of creative productivity. Having confidence in who we are and why we matter prepares us to actualize more of our potential by creating a complex, rich web of relationships. These possibilities are richer than ever before in our globally linked, mobile world.

In *Networking Smart*, Wayne Baker states, "The term

networking elicits strong feelings, positive and negative; some people swear by it, others swear at it." The approach you'll learn in *Your Network Is Your Net Worth* throws many of the existing ideas about networking out the window. If you are willing to focus first on your passions and purpose, I will show you how to reorganize your networking methods, as well as your entire life, around your true beliefs. When you do this, you will discover the kinds of lasting relationships, personal transformation, and, ultimately, tangible wealth that are the only foundations for happiness and success.

If this approach seems overwhelming or foreign, don't worry. Most likely, you are adapting to the digital and social evolution and you can thrive with a values-based, transformational approach to networking. The core of the approach is looking inside first, outside second. This approach to connecting should not feel like work; instead, it should be life-enhancing and collaborative and ultimately bring you joy and greater prosperity.

Connecting with others with similar values and passions can also increase your feelings of happiness in most cases. An article in *Scientific American* titled "Your Brain on *Facebook:* Bigger Social Networks Expand the Size of Neural Networks" by Gary Stix noted, "Lots of 'friends' drive the growth of gray matter in areas linked to processing social information." James Fowler, a professor at UC San Diego, stated in an interview with NPR, "We find that people at the center of the social network tend to be happier. . . . We think the reason why is because those in the center are more susceptible to the waves of happiness that spread throughout the network."

Connecting and building my network have changed my life. Because of the lessons I've learned, I have more friends than I ever imagined possible. I have thousands of Twitter followers and unlimited business contacts, and I'm more productive than ever.

What happened? I turned my weaknesses into opportunities for personal growth. I built my personal brand and started sharing my opinions.

If you are thinking "I'm not like you" or if connecting overwhelms you, you're not alone. Networking wasn't always easy for me. When I was younger, I used to hide behind a wineglass and would avoid gatherings if I didn't feel perfect. In my twenties, I'd stare glassy-eyed at Lifetime docudramas for hours on end, a cone of Ben & Jerry's in one hand and a cocktail in the other. But then I began to change my life. When I hit thirty, I started first to identify the habits of mind and actions that were holding me back. With self-reflection, practice, and focus, I learned how to authentically connect and build my social capital.

In my story, the straw that broke the camel's back was a heated argument with a boyfriend at a Halloween party seventeen years ago. I was drunk. He was late. What happened next included an argument, and the end of the night wasn't pretty. At that point, I did a lot of soul-searching. I went to therapy, and I made changes. It wasn't always easy, but it's always been worth it. I had to first learn to value myself and understand the importance of my interests and passions. I had to turn off the docudramas, and I dropped the cocktails. You don't necessarily need to toss out your Jack Daniel's to sharpen your connection skills, but you must understand what is holding you back, because if you're not where you want to be, an honest assessment of the reasons why should come first.

Your path to transformational networking may not be as dramatic as mine, but chances are you'll relate to some if not my entire story. *Your Network Is Your Net Worth* details the lessons and skills I have learned on my journey and in twenty-plus years of work experience, rising from an intern to the general manager of an advertising agency and from my post as vice president of marketing at Virgin America to an in-demand consultant and writer. In addition to my own experience, in this book are inspiring stories about a twenty-year Internet entrepreneur, a military wife, a film director, a young woman battling leukemia, a philanthropist, the CEO of a Major League Baseball team, a politician with dyslexia, a celebrity chef, an art gallery owner, and more.

In *Your Network Is Your Net Worth*, you will learn how to (1) develop a transformational attitude, (2) build a values-based team, and (3) cultivate fields of creativity. I hope my book and my approach to networking will inspire you to transform the way you make connections and help you thrive for years to come.

In the first part, I will show you how you can transform your networking by *developing a transformational attitude*. It introduces five core concepts: finding an authentic foundation, defining a purpose with the Funnel Test, networking with positive productivity, having a Give Give Get attitude, and the benefits of shaking it up. This section focuses on strengthening your inner confidence and self-esteem so you can nurture stronger values-based relationships.

In the second part, you will learn about *building a values-based team*. It introduces four concepts: using three degrees of separation, building your core circle, identifying power pockets, and connecting with hub players. This part details how technology has changed how we communicate, exponentially raising the rate of our interactions and reducing the degree of separation between connections. It shows why unlocking the power of connections is not a solo pursuit but one where you can benefit from understanding the dynamics of your core and secondary relationships.

The final section of *Your Network Is Your Net Worth* includes four chapters designed to help you *cultivate fields of creativity*, thus transforming your networking success. This section shows how everyone is a producer, the power of reaching critical mass, the ask, and how to know what is most important, your head, heart, or wallet.

I hope *Your Network Is Your Net Worth* will help you find the happiness, focus, prosperity, and success that I have found. Whether you're looking to improve your connecting skills or secure a new job or just want to understand the benefits of social media, this book is filled with stories, exercises, and tips to help you flourish in today's evolving world. Remember, building and strengthening your network will help you improve your happiness, productivity, and true net worth. In this global, networked economy, don't let your social capital lie dormant. Reinvest it!

Part I

The privilege of a lifetime is to become who you truly are.
—C. G. JUNG

I

Find Your Authentic Foundation

To Discover Where to Go, Know What's Holding You Back

Transform your networking by assessing the thoughts and behaviors that are holding you back. Do you need to break a habit or routine? What is keeping you from connecting or reaching your goals?

On a spring day in 2012, a former coworker named Jennifer Larson and I met at an Italian eatery to chat about life and business. With a smile she said, "The old Jen smoked, and her job was to clean the crap, including Cheetos, out of people's keyboards when their PCs were stuck. The old Jen went to bars wearing jeans two sizes too big and oversized shirts and a pager on her belt. The new Jen is a runner, has a great marketing job at Visa, and is working on her own start-up."

To put it mildly, Jen's transformation has been remarkable. I first met Jen five years ago, when I poached her from the IT department at Virgin America. We shared many closed-door discussions about career paths and job titles, but ultimately Jen's success resulted because she eliminated the barriers that were holding her back and defined her passions. Now Jen networks confidently, builds relationships, and works on projects that just several years ago were beyond her wildest dreams.

She explained, "I was always the principal's daughter. In college, I had freedom, there were cute boys, lots of beer, and I worked hard but not hard enough. I decided that the first class I received an A in would be my major. I ended up graduating in management information systems." After college, Jen took a job in IT at Frontier Airlines, where she was going to stay for six months. "I left seven and half years later. I was working too much. I didn't take care of myself, and I didn't feel good mentally. My path didn't feel right."

Next Jen joined the start-up team at Virgin America. "There were all these displaced people. It was a wild ride. I was still in IT and used smoking as a way to network with the guys and to get answers. But I felt my situation still fell short of my expectations for myself," she told me. Just after the launch, Jen joined my team in marketing. "I noticed people were a little edgier, put together, and I was forced to be social on many of my projects. I put down the cigarettes, signed up for a half marathon, and decided there was no reason for me to treat my body that way again," she explained. Her focus on fitness continued, and she did a race "where I ran 13.7 miles, climbed two peaks in Squaw Valley, jumped headfirst into an ice bath, climbed through mud, and did an obstacle course." Jen realized, "I was sleeping better. I felt like I fit in. I was energized, and I think endorphins had a role."

After five years at Virgin, Jen left for a new position to spread her wings. "In hindsight, I realize how great my experiences have been and how much I've learned. I now have balance, and I'm even working on a start-up outside of work." She shared the story of calling a past coworker, Sarah, for brunch. "We talked for three and half hours about innovation and business." The next day the contact sent Jen an invitation to a Harvard Business School Business Plan Contest where people were pitching business concepts for funding. "I put on a black wrap dress and grabbed a yellow purse. It was a color that gave me confidence and helped me stand out. I kept my head up, made eye contact, and had a goal to talk to at least five people," she said. She left the event with numerous business cards and later connected with new contacts from the event. "Now I always talk to people and ask for help. The worst thing that can happen is that they can say no," she told me with a smile.

Your Network Is Your Net Worth is about Jen, about me, about you, about your friends, and even about your neighbor. Your first step in this new way of networking is to assess and define the barriers that are holding you back. Jen put down the cigarettes, picked up running shoes, and found a confidence within that gave her the strength to shed the limits of her old identity.

In the old model of networking, Jen might have stayed in IT and focused her sights on climbing the rungs of her department ladder. The goal of old networking was a transactional meeting, not a transformational process. For example, career growth happened when a superior left the company and vacated a seat, not because of personal growth. If the wait for a promotion was too long, one might have dusted off a résumé or tried to make a move. The new model of networking, as in Jen's story, is based on a foundation of self-discovery and the pursuit of long-term relationships based on shared values and mutual interests and not on changes happening at your office or with superiors.

In the new model you connect via values and interests—not job titles—to build stronger, more productive, and more relevant relationships. In fact, job titles are often irrelevant. Today's intern might be tomorrow's CEO. As a result, it's very important to treat people respectfully and do your best not to burn bridges.

Consider my connection to Dennis Crowley, the founder of Foursquare, a location-based mobile company with more than a hundred employees and millions of users around the globe.

When I met Dennis at a conference in Tahoe, I learned that we had overlapped working at the same advertising agency. As he described it, "I read the Snapple fan mail and was the first new media hire in the New York office." I was the general manager of the San Francisco office right around the same time. In the age of transformational networking you are more likely to run into someone you've worked with under unpredictable circumstances, so always remember to treat your contacts as equals and respectfully.

In this chapter you will take an inventory and assess the barriers that are holding you back from achieving your personal and professional goals, a process I call creating an authentic foundation. If you're like me, finding your foundation will require some moderate shifts in conduct and planning. Other changes may be larger and more complicated as you remap attitudes and behaviors that require renewed attention, focus, and self-awareness. Through the process, you will develop a list of your potential barriers. If you have a long list, don't worry. Just focus on one at a time.

Common challenges include addiction, loss of self-esteem due to unemployment or taking time off to raise children, fear of change, feeling anxious over one's physical appearance, financial problems, social awkwardness, and so forth. Addressing them will help you experience positive change and make connecting with others an easier and more enjoyable process. Before we begin, I want to share a bit about my background and some of the barrier breaking I did to get where I am today. My barriers included:

- Using alcohol for escape
- Having feelings of being "less than"
- Never asking for help from others
- Battling periods of depression

I worked hard to break those barriers, and you can break yours too. To give you a little more background, I'm a regular girl who was born in Minnesota to a probation officer mom and an industrial designer dad. Neither of my parents talked about networking or the power of relationships. My mom was fanatical about sending thank-you notes and always said, "Education is important," but we never talked about the value of people in your network or how to make it in a competitive world.

My parents divorced when I was five, and my mom married a man who spent most of his time in his La-Z-Boy chair. My own dad, when I saw him, sat, day after day, at a drafting table drawing oddities. He was creatively content but not financially focused. He had a penchant for patents but died without a dime. He designed toy building blocks, a floating calf feeder, a swivel chair, a snowplow, and a plastic device you could put on a motorboat so your beer wouldn't spill.

Thanks to my mom's frugality and a grandfather who did well in business, I was able, at the age of eighteen, to move east to attend Boston University. If you are one of those people whose friendships date back to college or if you're the first to sign up to attend your high school reunion, that's not me. When I was younger, my world was small. I wanted to break out, but I had an overwhelming fear of meeting new people and always felt inadequate in some way.

Academically, I did okay, but I wasn't a superstar student. I wasn't an athlete. I wasn't skinny. I wasn't Jewish. I wasn't Catholic. I didn't know where or how to fit in. Rather than asking for help in college, I simply stuck to my arbitrary goal of finishing in four years because I convinced myself that this was what everybody did and if you didn't you'd be seen as a failure. The idea that my potential classmates might support me or that I could support them in the future didn't occur to me.

It's hard to say why I had so many barriers, but I'm quite sure a history of alcoholism ran in my family. Growing up I also recall some chaotic times: there were multiple divorces, our house burned down, fights erupted between my two older step-siblings, I became a regular underage drinker, and the entire family used the television to escape. That aside, I believe strongly that every situation provides an opportunity for learning. Without the barriers and hurdles, I might not have taken the inner journey to find my true self.

In the past, I didn't have the self-awareness to realize that I was the one holding myself back. My barriers were self-inflicted and self-perpetuating. Pouring out the cheap chardonnay was the first step to removing a barrier that stood in the way of my ability to connect to others and to be the architect of my own happiness. I went through many years of self-discovery during college and beyond, deliberately doing a lot of barrier breaking over the years, and my life has changed dramatically because of that.

Another barrier that I've worked to overcome is a mind-set of "feeling less than." I recall a time when I dated a journalist who had a charming habit of reading the dictionary and putting a red dot near every new word he read. But charm aside, his literary book club friends intimidated me. I convinced myself that he and his friends were smarter than I was. If I could turn back the clock, I would see a book club gathering as a perfect opportunity to learn about unknown authors or topics. If you change your perspective, overwhelming situations can be transformed into learning opportunities—as it was for me back then, but I didn't see it that way. Now when I experience negative thinking, I take a walk, read, or lounge in the bath, which helps to reset my point of view.

Or perhaps you can identify with a story shared by Matt Van Horn, an executive at the social media company Path. Several years ago, Matt had just moved to the Bay Area and he attended a networking happy hour. "I remember feeling very shy. I felt like an outsider," said Matt. He called his wife and said, "I want to come home; I am not enjoying myself," and she said, "Get out there and meet people, have a glass of wine, and don't come home until you have ten business cards."

Matt followed his wife's advice and started approaching people. By the end of the night, he had ten cards in hand and four follow-up meetings planned. He didn't let his inner voice hold him back, and he turned what could have been a missed opportunity into a valuable evening.

Regardless of if you want to make major or minor shifts in your networking, it's important to learn to work outside your comfort zone and explore uncharted situations. Take action, start a conversation when you're feeling uncomfortable, or ask someone to join an activity: the results may happily surprise you.

Step 1: Assess the barriers that are holding you back.

In Step 1, you will complete three exercises. The first is an exercise called "old conversation/new conversation"; the second is creating a "barrier list"; the third is sharing your list with a trusted friend or adviser.

Throughout *Your Network Is Your Net Worth*, I provide optional "tune-up tips" that you can do at your leisure. There are also sample exercises in Chapter 14 that have been completed by others who are looking to build or improve their networks. These can be reviewed for direction as you complete your steps and exercises.

Exercise 1: Write your old conversation (old self-perception or attitude) and new conversation (desired self-perception and attitude).

Begin your journey toward authenticity by completing the exercise we call old conversation/new conversation. Your "old conversation" consists of any negative thinking or attitudes you'd like to remove. Ask yourself, "What is holding me back from meeting new people and breaking out of my routine and limitations?" Grab a journal or a notebook and write down any negative statements that come to mind. It may seem odd to write down your thoughts and feelings, but do not worry—there are no right or wrong answers. Consider these examples of old conversations:

- I don't want people to feel sorry for me.
- I'm not good (smart, pretty, etc.) enough.
- I don't know what to say.
- I don't have the right experience or training.
- I don't have time or money to meet people.

Writing down fearful and anxiety-provoking thoughts helps us become conscious of and identify hardwired reactions that feed our negative self-talk; by writing down those fears, we become more aware of their origins and their effects on us. By talking to others about a negative issue, setting a positive goal, and working toward that goal by tracking our actions, we introduce behavioral change.

Then, when you're ready, shift into a new conversation. The "new conversation" list should focus on your positive qualities and aspirations. Ask yourself, "What qualities do I have or want to have that will help me meet people and expand my opportunities for change?" Write down your positive current and desired new conversations, desired attitudes, or desired behaviors, such as:

- I'm a great conversationalist.
- People like being around me.
- I have insights and ideas that can help others.
- My life is full of relationships that bring me joy.
- I deserve and am worthy of making new connections.

The next exercise in transformational networking involves taking an inventory of wasteful behaviors that soothe your pain in the short term but mask the underlying challenges that expand over time. Consider Jen's smoking or my drinking and how our addictions limited our ability to connect and network with our peers. The first step we both had to take was to acknowledge those habits as barriers. There are two types of barriers: those that you can change and modify on your own and those that may require more work and guidance from others. Before you make your list, here are some true stories of individuals and the barriers they overcame to reboot their lives with authenticity.

Addiction: From Homeless to Helpful, the Power of InvisiblePeople.TV

From 1990 to 1994, Mark Horvath was on the production side of the television business, responsible for getting *Wheel of Fortune* and *Jeopardy* to your television set. "I never met Vanna White, but I had a good job. But after twenty years of bad decisions and drinking and doing drugs I ended up homeless on Hollywood Boulevard." Prior to losing his job, Mr. Horvath was the director of distribution services at Starcom Television Services. He managed a film and video vault, was in charge of a fleet of drivers, and managed a duplication lab. Mr. Horvath, who is known on Twitter as @hardlynormal, related that after he was let go, he ended up homeless in front of Grauman's Chinese Theatre, with his six-foot iguana named Dog on his back. "I was suicidal and scared. It's hard to describe the hopelessness I felt. My head was buried in my hands, and my elbows were on my knees. I thought I'd have to deal drugs, beat up little old ladies and take their purses, or turn tricks. I never wanted to be homeless."

Mr. Horvath added, "At that moment, a bus of Asian tourists circled me and asked if they could photograph Dog. Without looking up I said, 'For a dollar,' and they all held out dollar bills. And after that, that's how I survived. I became the Lizard Man of Hollywood Boulevard. It was crazy."

Soon after, a church took Mr. Horvath in, and he lived there for eight years throughout his recovery. He went to Alcoholics Anonymous, to church, and back to school to study psychology, all of which helped him rebuild his life. He said, "I was a garbage head. My favorite drug was whatever you had. I'd swallow the pills and then ask what they were. After I got sober and I went from being homeless to having a credit score of 780, it was amazing." But in November 2007, Mr. Horvath lost his job when the recession hit. "I was hurting, depressed, and scared I'd be homeless again. Then I saw this book called *Finding Grace* that was filled with black-and-white photographs of homeless people. I thought, 'I could do that.' I always say, 'Don't waste a crisis,' so I grabbed an old camera and started a video blog on homeless people."

At the time, Mr. Horvath was looking for employment but kept focused on empowering homeless people in his blog InvisiblePeople.TV. "It helps me, and it helped put my problems in perspective. Then I started using Twitter to bring people with me on my journeys. I was eating dollar pizzas from Ralph's, getting feedback from people, and the miracles started to happen," he said.

In Baton Rouge, a tugboat operator shared a story about fifty homeless kids without shoes, and donations of shoes poured in. In Arkansas, a farmer donated forty acres of land that is now used to feed 150 people a week. And in Calgary, a fifty-eight-year-old homeless man with cancer was reunited with his family and spent his last thirty-three days with them before he passed away. Mr. Horvath now works at a homeless shelter during the day and works on his blog and video efforts in his spare time. He's also a frequent speaker, was invited to provide a keynote speech at the Geneva Forum on Social Change, and his efforts were featured on the YouTube home page. I asked Mr. Horvath why he believes his efforts have made an impact. "I try to give people my positive intention," he said, "and I share stories in an authentic way. I don't look at the people as homeless; I look at them as friends." He added, "No matter what is going on in my life, if I'm of service things stay in perspective."

Mr. Horvath has also turned down lucrative work. "I don't want to sit at a desk if I can help people get off the streets. Everything matters. We need to be human, be real, and treat every day like it's the Super Bowl. I'll keep doing this until the day it stops having an impact," he said.

Mr. Horvath addressed the barriers that were standing in his way and built a network and community to support his passions and purpose.

Self-Limiting Thoughts: Raise Your Bar, and Don't Let Age Be a Barrier

Suhail Doshi's story is radically different than Mr. Horvath's, but it also demonstrates how our own thinking or actions are often our greatest barriers to success. In 2006, Mr. Doshi enrolled at Arizona State University and started working on an undergraduate degree. "I went to ASU because it was cheap and I didn't want to burden my parents. My assumption was that the undergraduate school you attended didn't matter. I'd get good grades and then would try to get into Stanford to get a master's degree. I figured I'd be an electrical engineer, would get an entry-level job at Intel for $90K, and would work my way up from there." But immediately he knew that ASU was the wrong environment for his studies. "My assumptions were my own barriers, and I started to realize that I had set my bar too low. People around you can perpetuate your beliefs, but you can do anything if you're ambitious and work harder."

In August 2006, Mr. Doshi read a *BusinessWeek* cover story called "How This Kid Made $60 Million in 18 Months." The story concerned the Internet entrepreneur and Digg.com founder Kevin Rose. In that moment, Mr. Doshi reset his bar and decided, "I want to do that. It was a wake-up call. I didn't want to sit in front of a computer all day, I want to build things." He described how he would rush through his homework "as fast as possible" so he could work on his passion projects. While in school, he said, "I made every mistake I could, and I cared about stupid things. Sometimes I dropped projects too soon as I was trying to chase a gold rush. I learned that execution is everything and commitment means a lot."

He also learned that there was an inverse correlation between the number of projects he was launching and his grades at university. "Indian parents don't like you getting Cs and Ds; my parents were supportive, but my grades were dipping, and it was really depressing." Mr. Doshi kept building projects and launched everything from a site he described as the "Wikipedia of opinions" to apps called Super Fortune Cookie! and The Verb.

In May 2008, his career took a fateful turn when he interned at Slide, a company founded by Max Levchin, the former CTO and cofounder of PayPal. "At Slide, I wanted to test if the world would reward hard work or if life is really political and bureaucratic," he said. Over time, Mr. Levchin started to take notice of the work Mr. Doshi was doing with a product manager named Adora Cheung. "One day at an all-hands meeting, Max said, 'You should take a look at Slide TV and see what Adora and Suhail are working on.' I realized he was taking notice," said Mr. Doshi. Over the course of the internship, Mr. Doshi pitched several ideas to Mr. Levchin, and he learned that they both found joy in "cracking applications and breaking games" and that they both knew a low-level programming language called Assembly. "He became my biggest mentor. I've learned a lot from him, and he's always there for me," added Mr. Doshi.

In 2009, Mr. Doshi turned down a full-time opportunity at Slide and decided to take a leave from university. He launched an analytics platform for Web and mobile called Mixpanel, where he now employs thirteen employees, has raised $11.75 million and is running a profitable company. "I started this company when I was twenty. I wasn't of legal age to drink, but it felt natural to start a business. I had nothing to lose, and my confidence built over time. I try to empower people and delegate, and I know interns are valuable. You should never think you're better than them, since soon they might be running a company."

Mr. Levchin is an angel investor in and adviser to Mr. Doshi's company. "I think Max is the best angel investor in the Silicon Valley; if he invests in you, he'll do anything for you. I realize now my reward for my hard work at Slide was the relationship I built with Max."

Physical Barriers: From Nerd to Male Model

Another barrier to finding your authentic self comes from choices you make about your physical fitness, well-being, and personal appearance. Experts tell us that carrying a great deal of extra weight or ignoring a chronic health condition will manifest itself in a range of psychological and health implications ranging from shame and embarrassment to lack of energy, distracting you from your daily work and longer-term goals. They can also impede your personal and business relationships if you act out in anger or despair from the effects of your untreated issues (think of chronic back pain, high blood pressure, and headaches, as well as being overweight). First impressions matter, but what's more important is to feel confident and happy about who you are on the inside and out. Losing five or ten pounds isn't necessarily going to be easy or magically change your life, but learning to love yourself and adopting healthy lifestyle decisions can turn a half-empty glass into a half-full one.

Stefan Pinto, a self-described "overweight nerd turned fitness addict and male model" and the author of *Fat to Fit: 50 Easy Ways to Lose Weight*, shares his own unrecognizable before and after photos on his website. He says, "In 2001, the only vegetable I used to eat was ketchup; I changed my life by eating right and working out." He was inspired to change his life when a gym manager called him after the 9/11 attacks. "I had moved to New Jersey and joined a new gym but hadn't gone in months. The membership director called me to ask if I was okay. It was such a sincere act for a stranger to make that I went back. In many ways, the call changed me, but I was also ready for it," he explained. Mr. Pinto dropped sixty pounds and went from being a junk-food addict battling depression and numerous ailments to an inspirational role model with a washboard stomach. His transformation was so remarkable that his journey landed him extra roles on *CSI: Miami* and *Burn Notice*, modeling work in a billboard advertisement for a yogurt company, and placement in the centerfold spread of *Playgirl*. The magazine dubbed him "the perfect man."

Mr. Pinto and I met virtually on Facebook. I saw his posts and was intrigued that he was using the online community to coach others on weight loss techniques and mindful eating, so I sent him a message and we arranged to have coffee. I asked Mr. Pinto why he likes helping others, and he said, "I want to say I did something that affected people, life isn't just about passing time. The purpose of time is to teach. I've been in a pot that was outgrown. You can either stay and wither or get a bigger pot. When you make a change, it takes time for the roots to catch, but I'm willing to take that chance. I hope people I teach can create great change too." He added, "I encourage people to get fit but also to look at their individuality, as it is what will set you apart and set you free. You need to really love yourself. You don't want to wake up twenty years from now and say, 'Who the hell am I?' It's an inward journey, and I'm honored I can be a teacher."

Your healthy lifestyle and fitness goals may not be as ambitious as Mr. Pinto's, and the paths to attaining goals are always unique to the individual. For example, in my path to self-improvement, I've read up on superfoods, toxin flushing, fitness, and frankly anything else that would ease my mind and help eliminate fearful thinking. I've also learned that I'm my own worst enemy. I recall having a phone conversation with a successful businessman I dated from Los Angeles. I was at my desk working, and he was on his way to a Pilates class. "I wish I could go to Pilates," I said. "You can," he responded. He was exactly right. The only person holding me back from working out was me. Think about that as you look at your barrier list. Are you holding yourself back from moving forward? Are you your own worst enemy? Now is the time to look at your behavior and shift your thinking and actions into positive behaviors.

Tune-up Tip: Make a list of physical improvement goals.

Can you make a list of five fitness or physical goals? Achieving them will help build your confidence and help you abolish self-limiting behaviors. You'll be surprised how quickly new fitness routines and sports provide a path to confidence building and new friendships. Here is my first list of five physical improvement goals:

- Work out five days a week for at least forty minutes a day.
- Improve midsection and attempt to stop rear end from sliding to China.
- Incorporate mother/daughter fitness activities into weekend plans.
- Increase vegetable and protein intake.
- Use the StairMaster that has turned into a laundry hook in my garage.

Psychological Barrier: Finding a Voice

A barrier nineteen-year-old Rigo Estrada faced was a fear of public speaking. "A few years back I could be described as a meek and mild-mannered Clark Kent, without the superpowers to deal with the baddies. In the past, approaching others or opening doors was very difficult," he said. But Rigo, like many others, conquered his fear by addressing it head-on and by working with a mentor. "When I first met Rigo he wouldn't look me in the eyes or even answer me to say 'No.' He didn't feel what he had to say was valuable," said his mentor, Nancy Gale, who shares my last name but is not related. "Every week I worked with him, and he went from not talking to becoming our star student; he ultimately gave a brilliant speech in front of five hundred of his peers."

"Nancy had me make a video to send to Ellen DeGeneres to tell her about our program. I stuttered, stumbled, and stammered incoherently. But afterwards I felt an amazing glow," said Rigo. Gale added, "We had long talks about resilience and perseverance, and he started to understand that people he believed lived in white-picket-fence worlds also had challenges and that they may be different but we all face them."

Rigo was part of an entrepreneurial program for underprivileged youths called In True Fashion, where successful business leaders visit the classroom and share their authentic and personal stories. "We've had people talk about accidents, eating disorders, extreme dyslexia, and I myself have shared the story of being raped and also losing my mother to murder. There is something so real and genuine about stories. When a guest makes that kind of connection, the kids believe they can do whatever they want and whatever that person did," said Gale. (Nancy has mentored a number of students, some of whose stories I'll introduce in future chapters.)

Since Rigo made the first video, he has graduated from high school and started college full-time at California State University, Dominguez Hills. "Conquering my fear has allowed me to connect with students, and I now speak up when I need help or financial aid," added Rigo, the first in his family of immigrants from Central America to attend college. Gale noted, "Rigo made so much progress that he became our spokesperson, and we also gave him our first scholarship in honor of my mom. She was a mentor herself. She'd be proud of him, as he's really stepped up and has found his own voice."

Emotional Instability: A Father's Roller-Coaster Ride

My father was a brilliant designer, but I am convinced that had he lived today he would have been diagnosed as a manic-depressive. My father experienced high high highs and low low lows. He had extreme bouts of creativity followed by destructive lows, which my mother referred to as "his dark moods." He would be wildly creative one minute and completely withdrawn the next. He could not save or keep a penny in his pocket. When I was four, he did have one successful design run, which included creating a snow blower for the Toro Company and some other molded-plastic products. From that small windfall he went on to build an enormous house with an indoor swimming pool, an indoor basketball court, an in-law unit, a spiral staircase, an oversized garage, and more. He lost it all, including his temper and his marriage to my mother. During one infamous rage, my father took a sledgehammer to several cars belonging to people attending a neighbor's party because they were parked in our large circular driveway. In retrospect I see that my father's manic tendencies were directly linked to his reckless behavior with money.

Too often, people allow an unhealthy relationship with money, either overspending or a fear of financial insecurity, to stand in the way of their dreams and achievements. When he passed away, my beloved father lived in a small house owned by his third wife, yet he drove a used Rolls-Royce and wore an ascot tie. My hypothesis is that if he had had the proper clinical care, he would have had a chance to break the barriers that kept him from reaching his full potential and kept him from making healthy relationships and connections. This is an example of a larger-scale barrier where advice from a medical professional would be recommended.

Exercise 2: Make a list of barriers.

In Exercise 2 you will write down specific barriers or behaviors that are holding you back. Barriers can be big, such as having an overwhelming fear of people, or small, such as an inner voice always saying "I can't," "It won't," or "I never." Below are some questions to help you start. One tip is to start each sentence with an "I" statement so your inventory is about your behavior and not the actions of others.

1. Do you have barriers that get in the way of your success and happiness?
2. Do you emotionally or physically want to change any behavior or improve your appearance?
3. Do you have any compulsive or addictive behaviors, or have others on more than one occasion singled any out?
4. Do you have any fears or phobias that keep you from activities?
5. Do you change jobs often or find yourself under- or unemployed?
6. Do you make excuses or not follow through?

The above questions should help spark your thinking. If you worry that you are suffering from depression, anxiety, or addiction, the Mayo Clinic website, at www.mayoclinic.com, offers a wealth of extremely easy to understand materials and self-assessments. Part of doing the inner work and breaking barriers is to know when you need to seek support or advice from others.

Now that you have your list of barriers, look at them often. Your path to self-improvement is your own, and it's up to you to take the actions you need to be the best you can be. If you focus on yourself first, meeting people and making new connections will become increasingly easier. As you may have gathered, barriers can be small or large. I hope my stories and the stories of others will help you realize your full inner potential so you can connect and network with others in a long-term, values-based way.

After a week or two of writing and thinking about your barriers, you may want to take a new step to move into transformational networking by having conversations with a trusted friend or family member about what you've found. To increase the benefits of cognitive behavior change, try to set goals and track them on a weekly basis. If you're willing to take this action, Exercise 3 will help you get there.

Exercise 3: Share your barrier list with a friend or adviser.

Once you know what's holding you back, create a list of actions to replace or rid yourself of behaviors and actions that are holding you back. If you need to lose weight, look at your diet and fitness routine. If you need to wean yourself off an email addiction, don't leave your cellular phone on your night table and commit to checking email only several times a day. Figure out what works for you, and focus on the goal of self-improvement and positive growth. Exercise 3:

1. Share your barrier list with a friend, mentor, or adviser.
2. Make a plan to change or eliminate the barriers standing in your way.
3. Obtain outside support or talk to a medical professional if needed.
4. Don't get overwhelmed; focus on one barrier at a time.
5. Celebrate your process and success as you go.

Breaking down barriers will help build your confidence and enable you to be more present for the exciting adventures that lie ahead. Last, remember that it's important to focus on yourself or your inner work first. As a friend said, "If you don't like who you are, take an honest, unvarnished look at yourself. Change what you have to. We are all capable of so much."

Chapter 1: Summary

Step 1: Assess the barriers that are holding you back.

Exercise 1. Write your old conversation (old self-perception or attitude) and new conversation (desired self-perception and attitude).

Tune-up Tip: Make a list of physical improvement goals.

Exercise 2. Make a list of barriers.

Exercise 3. Share your barrier list with a trusted friend or adviser.

Top Tips

1. Connect via values and interests, not job titles.
2. Seek outside support or professional advice if needed.
3. View obstacles as opportunities for growth.
4. Find your authentic voice.
5. Review your barrier list often.
6. Replace old behaviors with new actions and attitudes.
7. Reward yourself when you make progress.

2

The Funnel Test

Focus Your Passions, Then Define Your Purpose

With advancements in digital technology, the world is becoming more transparent, and you can't fake it till you make it anymore. With the Funnel Test you will review your passions and define a twenty-word purpose to anchor your networking and ultimately help you increase your happiness and prosperity.

Today, we're always on and always connecting. You know the physical and emotional states of folks in your network. You know their interests and how they spend their time. You uncover common connections, birthdays, and relationship statuses. It's a new model that has changed the extent and dimensions of our relationships. New modes of communication have changed the frequency, length, and type of communications used to connect. I heard one young man joke, "An entire relationship can start, happen, and end on text messages." Steven Pinker, an author and behavioral psychologist, has suggested that several factors, including the Internet and social media, are expanding the "circle of empathy" we experience as humans. He states, "Historically, we only experienced a tiny inner circle, tribe, village, or clan." The rise of technology has been one key to expanding our circles. Pinker notes, "Over history, one can see the circle of empathy expanding: from the village to the clan to the tribe to the nation to more recently to other races, both sexes, children, and even other species." He quotes experiments by the social psychologist Daniel Batson and others that "reading a person's words indeed leads to an increase in empathy, not just for that person, but also for the category that the person represents." Pinker shows us what this expanded framework of networking is leading to: greater empathy and connection with circles of people we previously would not have known.

What this means to your networking is significant. You can organize your network based on what matters to you and what you care about. You can build stronger, authentic, sustainable connections through numerous channels. You don't have to wait for a job interview or a first date to express your passion for the environment or sports. Whether it be a conference breakout panel, a profile post, photos mined via a Google search, or a blog entry, these activities all create and build the image of you. The next step in transformational networking is to define your core passions and purpose in an exercise that I have named the Funnel Test.

Funnel Test exercises will help you anchor your interests to create a focused purpose. Your passions and purpose will evolve with time, but defining your interests will help you be more effective and will help you understand your purpose and how it aligns with others', which is vital in the process of connecting and developing relationships.

The increase in the ways we connect has also magnified the feeling of intimacy we have with our contacts, some of it false and some of it real, as a person's daily life unfolds on social media through photos, updates, and video posts. We communicate and network twenty-four hours a day and seven days a week with social media and the Internet; therefore, it's important to know what you stand for and value. Before the late 1990s, your last visual memory of a friend or contact would have probably been of your last exchange in person. If you use social media, your last memory of a personal connection is more likely to be of an image posted on Facebook or a 140-character tweet. With that in mind, isn't it important for you to define what you're trying to achieve and what you enjoy?

Part of defining your purpose is to understand how you like to spend your time, the types of activities at which you excel, and what relationships bring you joy. When you understand the answers to those questions, it will be easier to cultivate new associations. For some of us, our passions and purpose are clear and well defined from a young age. For others, interests and focus will change over time. Regardless of when or how you find your purpose, the process of growth and discovery never ends.

Step 2: Define your core passions and purpose with the Funnel Test.

In Step 2, you will complete three exercises that I call the Funnel Test. You will identify your passions and sweet spot, define a tone, and write a twenty-word (or fewer) purpose. Before you start your Funnel Test, a diagram of the test and some samples and insight into how a Funnel Test impacts decision making are shown on the opposite page.

Sample Passions: From Baseball and Statistics to Fitness and Family

In your Funnel Test you can put a high priority on any type of passion, from family to fitness or education to the environment. For example, the book *Moneyball* by Michael Lewis profiles

The Funnel Test

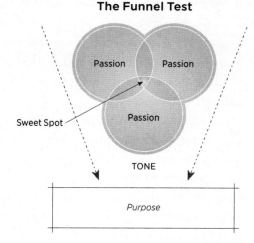

General Manager Billy Beane of the Oakland Athletics baseball team. It is clear from the outset that Mr. Beane's core passions are baseball, family, and statistics. It was the commitment to those passions that caused him to turn down the offer of a very large compensation package from the Boston Red Sox so he could stay in close proximity to his family. In a 2011 *New York Times* article he was asked if he had regrets, and he responded, "I have a wife and kids and parents who all live out here. If it was strictly driven by the desire to just win games, and if that was the end-all for me, then yes. But this is the type of environment [with the Oakland A's] I like and enjoy." Because Mr. Beane made decisions based on his values rather than just the potential financial gain, he focused on the things that mattered most to him, and no doubt the decision positively impacted his personal and professional relationships.

Closer to home, I watched my mother build a network based on her passions of volunteering, family, and fitness when, after having lived her entire life in Minnesota, she moved to California to be closer to her family. Within sixty days of arriving, my mother joined a master's swim team, found a group of women who played tennis at the park, and became an alternate in a golf foursome. When she added in volunteering for a single-mothers group and being a greeter at a local design show, her daily activities and calendar entries rivaled mine.

To give you a couple of additional examples, I've created hypothetical circles for Gertrude Stein, recently portrayed by Kathy Bates in the Oscar-nominated Woody Allen film *Midnight in Paris*. Ms. Stein was one of history's most successful networkers and was celebrated for her ability to bring twentieth-century artists and writers together in a salon environment that was instrumental in helping many artists build their careers and personal wealth. Her passion words might be art, community, and collecting.

For David LaPlante, a chief marketing officer who realized he was happier when surrounded by skiers and snowboarders, his passions might include skiing, technology, and people. Combining his passions and interests, Mr. LaPlante developed an annual conference called Snowcial that brings together digital influencers and snow fanatics for three days of dialogue peppered with poker games, ski outings, and late-night dancing.

My completed Funnel Test is shown on the opposite page. Can you see why I like writing about technology and people? Or why I am inspired by efforts that help people live more productive and healthier lives?

Based on my funnel, it's not surprising that one of the most rewarding jobs I had was being a documentary filmmaker. The films allowed me to tell stories, network, and meet a diverse group of people. In my case, I found my passion and an authentic personality in the late 1990s when I colaunched an effort called 2 Chicks, 2 Bikes, 1 Cause to raise breast cancer awareness among young women. With a friend named Donna Murphy, we created an integrated, educational multimedia campaign to raise funds for and awareness of the issue. We organized a 5,000-mile cross-country bike ride that we turned into a documentary we ultimately sold to Lifetime Television and Channel 4 in the United Kingdom. Along the bicycle journey we captured the stories of young breast cancer survivors and hosted events across the country. The effort received global coverage on *CNN Headline News*, *The Rosie O'Donnell Show*, and more. Taking a boost through technology, we partnered with Microsoft, which created a website and provided all technical back-end support. That breast cancer project, and my effort to write this book, mirror the passions and purpose listed in my Funnel Test. Now grab your journal, make a Funnel Test diagram, and define three of your passions. This is an exercise to help you find focus and clarity regarding activities and interests that bring you joy. This is not a do or don't list; it's a tool to help focus your intentions and networking efforts.

My Funnel Test

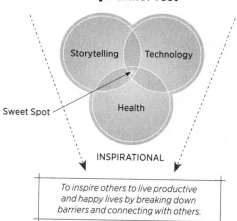

Storytelling

Technology

Sweet Spot

Health

INSPIRATIONAL

To inspire others to live productive and happy lives by breaking down barriers and connecting with others.

Exercise 1: Identify your personal passions.

In Exercise 1, fill in the three rings in the funnel with three of your passions. Don't worry, you can change the words in your funnel over time. Identify three passions or a succinct set of words that clearly defines your core interests.

The Funnel Test

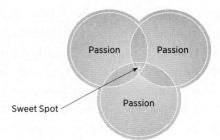

The area where your three passions overlap is your sweet spot. If you can find activities, work, or relationships that combine two or more of your core passions, you are likely to hit the jackpot and be more effective in and excited about your actions and activities. To spark your thinking, a list of questions and sample passions are listed below.

1. What are my strengths?
2. What are my weaknesses?
3. If I had a superpower, what would it be?
4. What activities bring me joy?

Sample Passions
Academics, acting, animals, architecture, art, aviation, athletics, cars, comedy, coaching, children, community, dancing, design, economics, entrepreneurialism, environment, family, fashion, finance, food,

gardening, health, history, inventing, mathematics, medicine, meditation, music, people, photography, politics, religion, romance, science, singing, spirituality, storytelling, teaching, technology, traveling, volunteering, wine, writing, yoga

Your last task in this exercise is to make a chart and write down how you are cultivating your passions. Grab your journal and make three columns, one for each passion. Make a commitment to improve, particularly where your involvement is limited. Let's say that if you're passionate about photography, make a commitment to go to photography exhibits several times a year and find online communities about the topic. For example, two of my goals are to take an improvisation class as a way to nurture my interest in storytelling and to go on weekly hikes with friends to support my passion for health. Below is an example of ways I plan to cultivate my passions.

Passion Goals Chart		
Storytelling Goals	Health Goals	Technology Goals
Take a comedy class	Train for a running race	Consult with tech start-ups
Finish my book	Hike/swim with friends	Read online tech dailies

In addition to investing in your passions, another benefit of defining your areas of interest is that you can share your opinions and thoughts on these topics with offline and online communities. You can also build your credibility around your passions using many of today's digital tools such as Twitter, Pinterest, Tumblr, Facebook, WordPress, and YouTube.

Before you define your tone and purpose, here are several stories of people who have put barriers aside and focused on their passions.

From Dishwasher to Award-Winning Chef:
Hard Work and Passion

Chef Michael Mina, an award-winning celebrity chef with eighteen restaurants, started in the industry at fifteen as a dishwasher and prep cook. Chef Mina noted, "Right away I liked the intensity of being in a restaurant. I was infatuated and fell in love with the whole feeling, it was like a family." By age sixteen, Chef Mina was working sixty to seventy hours a week in addition to going to school so he could "learn everything I could." One fateful day, Mr. Mina was watching *Lifestyles of the Rich and Famous* when the host, Robin Leach, was visiting Jeremiah Tower, a celebrity chef. Chef Mina recalled, "In the show, they were tasting sauces and drinking champagne and I knew that's what I wanted. I just had no idea I'd have to work so hard to get it."

Chef Mina, who was born in Cairo, lived in central Washington State when he decided to tell his parents he wanted to skip college to become a chef. "My father was not pleased. In Egypt you have three career choices: doctor, lawyer, or engineer. He said to me, 'You want to be a servant?' Finally we agreed that I would go to college for one year and if I still wanted to be a chef after that, we'd discuss it." Chef Mina began researching culinary schools and set his sights on getting more practical experience. "I moved to Seattle for college, and I talked my way into a job at the restaurant in the Space Needle. I was the least qualified of the applicants, but I made my way into the kitchen and struck up a conversation with the chef. Somehow I learned he liked bird hunting; we bonded because my parents lived on a property full of birds, and he offered me the job. It's odd how little conversations can change your life." After five months, Chef Mina's father started to realize that his son's passion wasn't going to disappear. "It's all I could talk about. One day my dad said, 'If you're going to do this. I want you to do it right. I've been researching, and you need to go to New York.'" With his parents' blessing, he left college, applied to the Culinary Institute of America (CIA) in New York, and was accepted.

Chef Mina's strong work ethic continued, and, he recalled, "I did everything I could to work and learn from the best chefs possible." One summer break, he went to California and kept visiting the Bel Air Hotel, because he dreamed of working for the chef, George Morrone. "I wanted to work with the best. I kept visiting the restaurant until I met a pastry chef that offered to give me a 'test run' and introduce me to George." His efforts paid off. "George has been a huge influence on me. He has been a true mentor and one of my best friends for twenty years."

After graduating from the CIA, Chef Mina followed Chef Morrone to San Francisco, and they opened a restaurant called Aqua. By age twenty-three, Mina was executive chef, and he recalls, "It was like being on center stage. We brought New York–style service to San Francisco. And now every person you see around me, they grew up with me in the business. We've all stayed together.

"My father was right; we are servants in this business. No matter how many television shows I've been on or famous people I've served, the reality is that as a chef it's your job to please people as soon as they walk in the door. There is an enormous amount of work that goes into this, but when you do things right and exceed expectations, it's very gratifying."

Tune-up Tip: Collect experiences, not just paychecks.

One transformational networking tip is to focus on your "journey" and passions, both personally and professionally, not just paychecks. Collecting experiential moments or having a "bucket list" (of activities you want to accomplish in your life) is a great way to keep your passions in the forefront.

A Purpose to Connect People: From Ham Radio to Voice over Internet Protocol and Beyond

Jeff Pulver, a technology entrepreneur, also follows his passions and purpose. In the midnineties, Jeff Pulver realized he was being fired from his job as vice president of information technologies at Cantor Fitzgerald in New York City when he attended a meeting and saw that his name wasn't on the organizational chart. "I had been there for eighteen months," he noted. "I raised my hand and said, 'I'm not on the org chart,' and my two bosses looked at each other and said, 'I thought you let him go.'" For Jeff it turned out to be a blessing in many ways.

Jeff, who went on to be a founder of Vonage and an Internet entrepreneur, shared how he continued to focus on his core passions and ultimate purpose to connect people when he lost his job. "Turning back the clock, when I was just nine my uncle took me to his office and showed me this little box with knobs. It was a moment that changed my life. He turned one of the knobs, said something cryptic, and then let go of the microphone. There was a roar of voices all waiting to talk. I was mesmerized. I was like— wow—my uncle had found the cure for loneliness. All I had to do was take the box, a ham radio, to my bedroom, and I'd have the solution."

By age twelve, Jeff had taught himself Morse code, learned all the rules and regulations of being a ham radio operator, and was on his way to building what he described as "my first social network." Jeff was so enthralled with the system that he often spent forty to sixty hours a week on ham radio while going to school. He was actively chatting with people around the globe through his teenage years, his twenties and beyond. "There were many people who were very meaningful that I never met; Sam in the Bronx, Joe from Boston, and people around the world. In the eighties there were even contests in the Soviet bloc to see who could talk to the most people in as many different countries as possible in a forty-eight-hour period."

One thing led to another, and Jeff started writing his own software to manage his ham radio contests. "It was too complicated to figure out an optimization matrix to know how many people I was talking to, so by fourteen, I was writing my own software." Against his wishes but with his parents' encouragement, Jeff enrolled in college and got an accounting degree. After college he started doing consulting work at an accounting firm but was bored. He started experimenting with what eventually became known as voice over Internet protocol. "In the early days of the Internet, at least twenty percent of the people were using ham radio call signals." After being let go by Cantor Fitzgerald, Jeff eventually started a company that became known as Vonage and sold that business on September 10, 2001, for "$57 million on paper." The next day terrorists attacked, and more than two-thirds of the people at Cantor Fitzgerald died when American Airlines flight 11 struck and destroyed the North Tower of the World Trade Center in New York City. "I was devastated and depressed, but I realized that losing my job saved my life," Jeff noted. Today he continues to be an Internet entrepreneur and investor in start-ups. He also curates and hosts social media conferences in cities around the globe.

But the kind of passion that drove Jeff since his adolescence does not, on its own, guarantee a $57 million payoff. You have to have a practical outlet to produce results, and you have to know how to get there. I believe it is important to first determine how you are going to articulate your passions and with what type of tone.

How We Message

During my time launching Virgin America, we used the phrase "fighting mediocrity" to create a mantra or tone around which the internal marketing team could come together. The phrase was a rallying cry to make everything better than the standard, staid category. It meant never settling for products, advertising, or anything relevant to the brand that was mediocre. From the colors of the headphones and availability of food on demand to being the first to have full-fleet Wi-Fi, this type of thinking reinvented the airline category—and it's the type of thinking you can use to raise your individual bar.

The tone I choose is *inspirational*. I wish to be inspired on a daily basis to learn and to connect with others. Tone is a driving force that connects you to the world. For example, I want to be an inspirational storyteller and also someone who is inspired by technology. I also want to strengthen my focus on good health, which I believe directly correlates with happiness.

Exercise 2: Define your tone.

For Exercise 2, think about how you want to present yourself to the world. What is your authentic voice? Are you quiet and reserved? Witty? Bold? Irreverent? To use the Gertrude Stein example again, I'd define her tone as *intellectual*. Billy Beane, the general manager of the Oakland Athletics, communicates with a *resourceful* tone. Now fill the space below your passion circles with a selected word for your tone. Like a funnel, where the contents flow from top to bottom, envision all of your actions being influenced by your tone. Remember, simple is good.

The Funnel Test

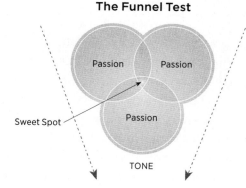

Sample Tones

Adventurous, ambitious, animated, assertive, caring, competent, confident, cooperative, democratic, dependable, direct, easygoing, eccentric, enthusiastic, giving, glamorous, honest, idealistic, independent, industrious, inspirational, intellectual, irreverent, resourceful, sensitive, sexy, shy, strong, unique, wild, witty, zany

In the last exercise of this chapter, you will streamline your passions and create a purpose statement. My recommendation is to keep this as simple as possible. Some brands and companies do this, and it also happens to be a valuable exercise for self-reflection for any individual. I've found that companies with lucid and succinctly described visions are more likely to succeed than those with unclear or highly complex visions. Imagine that you have five floors of elevator stops and you need to convince someone to hire you while you ride up together. Or you are given three minutes on a stage in front of your peers and you have to describe your personal mission. What would you say? How would you create a memorable connection?

Fred Reid, the founding chief executive officer of Virgin

America, shared with me how the airline's purpose, "To create an airline people love," was born: "I had written it on a paper and had thrown it into the trash. I initially thought it was too simplistic, but that *is* what we wanted to do. Can you imagine? Have an airline people loved?" After some deliberation, Reid and the founding team kept coming back to the simple phrase and decided it was the perfect mantra for the start-up that faced a complicated uphill battle prior to liftoff in 2007.

Ken Bieler, the director of engineering at Virgin America, told me how the simple phrase kept the team focused during the early years. "Every vendor we worked with told us our ideas couldn't be done. We kept pushing and challenging people. The airline was our baby, we focused on innovation and being an airline that people would love," he said. "It's hard to describe the passion people had and sacrifices we made to launch the airline." He explained that every person at the company was living the purpose.

Exercise 3: Develop a twenty-word (or fewer) purpose.

How would you talk about your own focused goals? What do you want to accomplish in life? And work? Write what is in your gut, and look at the passion words in your Funnel Test. Here are some samples to get you started. Your goal is to write a phrase of fewer than twenty words that describes your purpose:

- To have a thriving consulting business that helps nonprofits with philanthropy efforts.
- To launch a start-up technology business, which I can run remotely, that brings added value to the gaming industry.
- To promote new ideas in the green energy market in the environmental space, to reduce pollution and global warming so my kids will have a better future.

- To develop my skills as a comedian and support myself with my creative efforts.
- To show others ways to bring commerce and causes together to make a difference.

As shown in my Funnel Test, my purpose is *To inspire others to live productive and happy lives by breaking down barriers and connecting with others.* Here is my sample filled-in Funnel Test:

My Funnel Test

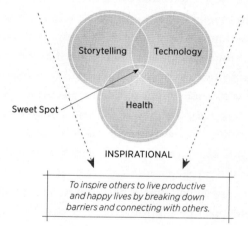

Now fill in your funnel and with your purpose in mind answer these questions in your journal:

1. Will my purpose bring me happiness?
2. Can I earn a living by focusing on my purpose?
3. Does my purpose support or conflict with my passions?
4. Does my purpose bring any greater good to the world or others?
5. Do I need to make any changes to start on the path to achieving my purpose?

6. Does my personality support my purpose?
7. What is blocking me from living my purpose?

Be the Best You Can Be

At this point, you may be thinking that your purpose is out of reach. For example, if your purpose is to be an actor, concerns about making enough income to put food on the table are going to be your constant companion. That is where the work comes in. Sometimes we have to make sacrifices or take baby steps in the short term to help us get to where we want to be. However, if you don't even know where you want to go, it will be quite hard to get there. I remember when I was laid off as general manager of an advertising agency in San Francisco, I went from a desk that looked like a command center to taking a freelance project while sitting in a gray cube helping a human resource team recruit media professionals. It wasn't my dream job, but I knew if I practiced what I ultimately called positive productivity, I was making progress—even if my steps were little ones at the time. I knew the reality of needing to pay bills. I had to put my ego and previous title aside and practice gratitude for the paycheck that arrived every two weeks.

Ultimately, the skills I learned recruiting other people helped me in my larger role at Virgin America. I better understood how to find good candidates, and I had created a larger network that served me well. Sometimes we gain more than expected, so try not to prejudge an opportunity. Stay optimistic, stay productive, and be the best you can be. Stay focused on your purpose, but know there is potential learning in every action.

A musician I know also shared some thoughts on being the best you can be: "I do remember reading about Communist China: that people sweeping the streets would often have a sense of satisfaction because they were making a contribution to society. I think whatever it is you do, you have to take seriously what your role is and do it as well as you can. The problem we have is that television and the Internet have brought the lives of the superwealthy right into the face of everybody. So people start thinking that is what happiness is. But happiness is really about loving what you do."

Tune-up Tip: Review your passions for passion-based revenue streams.

Look at your trio of passions and identify if you have revenue-generating goods or services to offer. For example, if you love cooking you might offer cake-baking services. Exchange sites, such as Zaarly, make it easier for people to buy and sell local services and goods to generate income and make connections. Identifying passion-based revenue streams will help make transitions and pivot points easier and more enjoyable to manage.

Where are you on this spectrum? Have you clearly identified your purpose? If you don't have a defined purpose, you will not be as productive in expanding your personal and professional relationships. So define your passion and purpose and use the last, optional tune-up tip in this chapter to keep your focus on track.

Remember, your passions, purpose, and career path may change over the years. In my professional life, I've been a waitress, worked at an advertising agency, been a filmmaker, directed commercials, worked for an airline, and written a book. My personal passions have evolved too. When defining your passions and purpose, the goal is to authentically define your interests and purpose at this moment in time. On any journey, you may change your course or find new sources of inspiration. Be purpose-based, but also aware, flexible, and realistic.

Tune-up Tip: Write a manifesto.

With your Funnel Test as a filter, reminding yourself daily to live with your passions and purpose in mind can be very helpful in fulfilling your goals. The tool I find most useful is a verbal manifesto or a prioritized list of mantras to sharpen and maintain my focus. A manifesto is a written, public declaration of the intention or views of an individual, group, or political party. I keep a manifesto that my sister gave me on my desk and look at it daily. Sample phrases from my manifesto include:

Make your own path. Never stop learning. Help people. Look at your goals every day. Collect experiences, not things. Simplicity is key. Believe in yourself. You have to put something out to get something back. Ignore doubters, especially when in your own head.

So take some time and write a manifesto. When you say a phrase out loud, it does help to make it real. For example, when I had just started writing this book, I ran into a neighbor who was walking his dog. "You're a schoolteacher, right?" he asked. I thought about it and responded, "Yes, but not at a school, I teach with stories in speeches and blogs." So share your passions, purpose, and plan: the more you live it, the more concrete and ingrained it will become in your relationships and activities.

Chapter 2: Summary

Step 2: Define your core passions and purpose with the Funnel Test.

Exercise 1. Identify your personal passions.

Tune-up Tip: Collect experiences, not just paychecks.

Exercise 2. Define your tone.

Exercise 3. Develop a twenty-word (or fewer) purpose.

Tune-up Tip: Review your passions for passion-based revenue streams.

Tune-up Tip: Write a manifesto.

Top Tips

1. Focus your passions and purpose to hone your networking skills.
2. Collect experiential moments and create a "bucket list" to keep your passions in the forefront.
3. Review your strengths and weaknesses.
4. Set the stage for dialogue with a defined tone.
5. Be the best you can be regardless of the task.
6. Visualize your Funnel Test as you make connections!
7. Remember that your passions and purpose can change over time.

3

Positive Productivity

Connect Purpose to Action

Positive productivity involves developing a mind-set of conscious effort to make the most of your time, connections, and relationships to increase your happiness, success, and true wealth.

In his book *Screw Business as Usual,* Sir Richard Branson wrote, "Ordinary people have enormous power—let them unleash it. . . . learn what you can do and—as NIKE would say—just do it." This chapter will explore ideas such as the impact of taking action, using pivot points for productivity, the role of mentors and collaboration, mixing business with pleasure, and how to say "no" to tasks that may lead you off your desired path. I call making a conscious effort to use your time efficiently and wisely being in a state of positive productivity.

To be in a positive productivity state, it is important to be aware of the barriers you have removed or are working to remove. For example, if you have significantly cut back on your television viewing, be careful and don't tune in to a new miniseries that could monopolize your evenings or weekends. If you overbook and leave too little time for your family, self-care, or your work responsibilities, your networking will result in thin, shaky connections.

Step 3: Create a mind-set of positive productivity.

In Step 3, you will create a Purpose Plan in Exercise 1. You will then do a Collaboration Review in Exercise 2 and a Time Waster Audit in Exercise 3.

Move into Action: Take Small Steps Toward Your Purpose Plan

We've all felt it: the moment of feeling hopelessly stuck or utterly uninspired and the fear that it will never pass. Dread. Lethargy. Tears. That moment can come unannounced and may seem to linger on its own terms. I can recall lounging in bed for an entire weekend without feeling inspired or motivated. I am sure you too have had moments of being overwhelmed by the size of an obstacle, and in my experience, a reliable way to deflate that feeling is to take a single step: one small one, followed by another.

In his book *Little Bets: How Breakthrough Ideas Emerge from Small Discoveries*, Peter Sims details how taking small steps is a great way to solve larger problems or find great opportunities. I experienced a perfect example of this when I climbed Mount Kilimanjaro. I remember waking up at moonrise to start the trek to the summit. It was cold and dark, and footing was often uneasy. I was traveling with a friend and a local guide named Zacharia, who kept repeating the Swahili phrase "Pole-pole," which means "Slowly, gently, quietly; be calm, take it quietly, don't excite yourself." Before I knew it, one step at a time, we had made it to the summit of Uhuru Peak, or "Freedom Peak" in English.

I spoke with Peter about *Little Bets*, and he said, "We often think we need to have ideas or projects figured out before we start, but that's not the best way to work." He explained that many comedians, companies such as Pixar, and even the famed architect Frank Gehry have segmented big projects into small, obtainable actions. Peter shared how the comedian Chris Rock worked for months in clubs, trying many of his ideas and jokes night after night, to determine what an audience would like or dislike. "By the time he gets to Letterman, he has his act fine-tuned and polished." So one step in finding positive productivity and creating a purpose plan is to not let the big picture over-whelm you. Look at the task at hand, from preparing a résumé to writing thank-you notes, and break the project down into digest-ible bits. Don't be discouraged if you don't have the answers all at once: move forward with small actions until you do.

For example, after a breakup several years ago, I wanted to stay home and sleep, but I knew I needed to find work to pay the bills. I was depressed at the time, but that period turned out to be one of the most growth-filled and transforming times of my life. At that low point, I was able to summon my positive productivity, which helped me build a network and land my job as vice presi-dent of marketing at Virgin America. I certainly shed tears and had sleepless nights, but I filled my days with tasks such as this:

- I was a real-people model in a Lands' End shoot.
- I edited a video for a friend's father's seventy-fifth birthday party.
- I did the laundry, made the beds, and went grocery shopping.
- I pitched an advertising project.
- I was picked to model in an ad for a software company.
- I directed commercials for Country Music Television.
- I interviewed for a job at a company and didn't get it.
- I updated my résumé and bio again.
- I helped a friend with a public relations project.
- I went running.
- I interviewed, interviewed, and interviewed.
- I didn't get a job that I wanted.

- I interviewed, interviewed, and interviewed.
- I was offered the job at Virgin America.

My productivity helped me meet new people, and I used my connecting skills to ask about potential jobs and opportunities. It was a contact from the Country Music Television gig who gave me the name of the recruiter managing the search for the Virgin America job. I worked my phone, email, and in-person connections daily. I told people I was looking for freelance or full-time work and followed up promptly. In less than five months, while consulting for several clients and doing real-people modeling to pay the bills, I landed a dream job, where I led a marketing department and met hundreds of people who have changed and expanded my world. When I needed it most, my network proved to be my net worth. Without my network, I would not have heard about the Virgin America job opportunity. Without my network, I would not have had the references (i.e., a prior employer and a past client) to provide to pass the employment screening process. Without my network, finding a job in a downturning economy could have been much more challenging.

Remember, *Your Network Is Your Net Worth* so don't burn bridges and when you have a setback, don't retreat! Expand your circle of friends and professional allies; focus on networking opportunities, and positive productivity will help turn obstacles into growth situations. This idea is simple. Remember: *In our global, networked economy, you can't allow your social capital to lie dormant. Reinvest it!* Become industrious, and you'll feel great and meet people. It's true. So each day, to get more energy, be productive and active, and you'll be unconsciously taking steps to build your future happiness. You'll be surprised at how much you can accomplish if you take one step a day toward a personal or networking goal that you are trying to achieve.

Tapping an Online Network: Market Your Bliss

One example of a person who moved closer to his purpose with a plan is Tom Fishburne, a Harvard-educated businessman who excelled in marketing but possessed a true passion for cartooning. He knew he wanted to build a life around it but didn't know how to turn cartooning into a business. After years of moonlighting as a cartoonist, he finally worked up the courage to leave a great job at a good company during a recession and decided to take his cartoon business, Marketoonist, to the next level. He knew the traditional cartoon business was dying with the decline of traditional newspaper sales, but his weekly online marketing cartoon was getting more than 100,000 readers a week. "It was hard to leave the safety net behind, but I had started to build a network of great potential clients online," he said. "It's incredibly fulfilling to have one hundred percent of my time, rather than nights and weekends, to dedicate to this business." Tom made the leap by tapping his network to gather enough freelance clients to generate 50 percent of his full-time salary, and he developed a concrete plan for how to reach his full salary within one year. By building an online network and having a plan, Tom had a step-by-step process and a network that helped turn his dream business into a reality. Tom's advice for others: "It's not enough to just follow your bliss, you have to learn how to market your bliss."

Maximizing Pivot Points: A Surf Lesson

Learning how to deal with transitions, or what I like to call "pivot points," is another facet of moving into positive productivity. Rachel Masters, a cofounder of Red Magnet Media, faced a pivot point in her career when she was fired after working for a company called Ning for two years. "I was shocked. I wasn't sure what to do but was fortunate that I had saved some money, so I decided to go to Bali." Rachel not only went to Bali, she also decided to attend a Surf Goddess Retreat. "I arrived, and there were seven women in one hut. After several days of bonding and a little alcohol, people started sharing stories. It really put things in perspective, as what I heard was a lot worse than my situation," she said. Rachel also told me, "On that trip one of the women wanted to go to fortune-tellers and healers, and I kept going with her. I'm not sure what happened, but one moment, I realized I didn't need someone to tell me my future. I can control my own destiny. I realized I'm in control."

After Rachel returned from her trip, she started her own digital media company and has landed projects with the bands Duran Duran and Linkin Park. "We're successful because we get stuff done. We don't just talk. We're smart, and we don't waste time or money. And we get great results." If, unlike Rachel, you are not in the position to travel to find your pivot point, I urge you to tap into your passions to find healthy, positive activities that you can schedule into your routine during a transition or undertake a project you have always dreamed of but never had the time to pursue. Start exploring ideas and activities that will bring you closer to your purpose. Times of change can yield extraordinary results in your effort to build new connections, so take full advantage of your pivot points.

Exercise 1: Create an action list or purpose plan.

On your path to networking success, you will encounter projects and tasks you need to complete to help you move toward your purpose. Perhaps you need to pull together a portfolio or writing samples. Or perhaps you want to convert a part of your apartment or home into a work area. Think about a project that you've wanted to start, and think of several small steps you can take to get started. Get out your journal and write several actions you can take to move toward your purpose. For example, when I decided I wanted to realize my passion for storytelling and write a book, here are several actions I took:

- I emailed writers in my network and asked for coffee dates.
- At the coffee dates, I asked for agent recommendations.
- I reviewed a sample book proposal.
- I wrote a proposal.
- And rewrote the proposal.
- I pitched agents and was turned down.
- I went to a writer's conference and met an agent.
- I sent my proposal to said agent from the conference.
- He agreed to take me on if I rewrote the proposal.
- I rewrote my proposal again.
- Nearly twenty publishing houses rejected my proposal.
- We secured several meetings and closed a publishing deal.

What actions can you take to move you closer to your passions, purpose, or goal? If you're committed to a project or purpose, don't let the no's stop you. Keep trying. Accept feedback. Keep what's working and throw out the rest. If you're really passionate and driven, do not give up.

The Power of Collaboration: A Key to Success

Another key to positive productivity is to surround yourself with people who are both smarter than you and open to collaboration. The new form of networking is not about climbing a ladder to success; it's about collaboration, cocreation, partnerships, and long-term values-based relationships. Jack Hidary, a successful entrepreneur, shared his view on why collaboration is so important. "I looked at how innovation has changed from the early 1900s to now, and one of the main differences is that innovations were often developed by a single individual in the past, and now breakthroughs tend to come from group collaboration." Supporting Jack's idea, consider that more than one person started Google, Twitter, and Instagram, a company purchased by Facebook for a billion dollars in cash and options before it celebrated its second anniversary. Or how Netflix created a contest with a $1 million prize for the team that could develop an algorithm to predict user ratings for films based on past ratings. Jack continued, "If we want to make positive change, we must trust and be open."

Often, collaboration is the glue that holds networking and connecting together. When we share ideas and work on projects as a group the results can be much greater than solo attempts. Jack added that through his program, National Lab Network, an effort that encourages experiential and group learning in K–12 schools, they have found that teamwork and group projects more closely mirror life. "Life is about solving problems and working with people," he said. "Memorizing facts and figures or climbing a solo ladder isn't how things work today."

One of the most productive groups I belong to is a Facebook group of writers who share values and interests. I often turn to the group to get advice or recommendations or simply to share thoughts. Finding groups to connect with is a great way to increase your positive productivity. One friend told me, "When building software, the more you share, the better it is. That's one reason folks in Silicon Valley are so excited, willing, and generous with their time and resources. We'll all be in the industry for twenty years, and what comes around goes around."

A Winning Combination: There's Magic Inside

Larry Baer, the CEO of the San Francisco Giants, shared several additional examples of the power of passion and collaboration. "For whatever reason, my DNA or my psychological underpinnings, I'm a people person. My friend Larry Lucchino, the CEO of the Red Sox, and I decided we're in the 'happy business.' I love seeing mothers and sons, father and daughters, and grandparents and grandchildren in the stadium. It's a generational business, and it's about community." Mr. Baer has always loved baseball. As a child, he says, he often ate his last spoon of ice cream quickly so he could leave the dinner table and put his transistor radio up to his ear to listen to the games. "Sometimes I hid under my covers and listened without my parents knowing."

In August 1992, when Mr. Baer was in the television business, the current owner of the team announced a purchase agreement to move the San Francisco Giants to Tampa for $118 million. Being a die-hard fan, Mr. Baer jumped into action. "Peter Magowan, who was running Safeway, and I gathered a team of eighteen civic-minded people including Bill Hewlett, Don Fisher, Charles Schwab, and other big names in business. We came together and assembled a $100 million bid, and somehow we talked the league into taking it," he said. "If you care enough, you can make things happen. It really was for the community, as back then baseball was a bit dead."

By 2010, Mr. Baer had been working for the Giants for years, and the team became the World Series champions. "Everything was working on all cylinders. It doesn't happen a lot in life, but it was clicking. The pitching was outstanding, there was clutch hitting, we were in a race, but we weren't worried about where we were going. The players were creating performances they had never done before, and no challenge felt insurmountable." He continued, "There was confidence, but not in an arrogant way; we just put our heads down and realized we could do anything. And we were feeding off adrenaline. When you see crowds of people with beards on, fake wigs, and panda hats, it is like you are on top of a volcano that is going to explode."

After the long-awaited win, the Giants were welcomed home with a parade, and more than a million fans greeted the team. "The game workers, ushers, security workers, and ticket takers, everybody marched in the parade. It was inclusive to the entire community. To receive love from over a million people, it was humbling. It was the highest high, and everybody's ship came home," said Mr. Baer. In 2012, the magic of team collaboration happened again and the San Francisco Giants took home another World Series title.

Exercise 2: Conduct a collaboration review.

Grab your journal and think about your defined purpose. Are there online or offline groups you should join to get closer to your goals? Have you been sharing your purpose with your network of contacts or thinking about it in a vacuum? If you need to become more skilled at collaboration, write down several groups you could join or a conference you might like to attend that will help you live your purpose.

Time Wasters: They All Add Up

As you consider new collaborations and joint endeavors, you also need to look at opportunities with your purpose and Funnel Test in mind. There is a fine line between productivity and frenzy. For example, productivity can be quickly drained if we let email or the Internet run our day rather than the other way around. If you have a ding or a pop-up screen when you get a new email or tweet, your productivity may ultimately suffer. One friend took several days to opt out of unwanted lists and spam and said, "I found a calming, Buddhist Nirvana from purging and moving away from all of the insanity. Now I only get a steady stream of the important stuff."

As with most powerful technologies, the Internet has many benefits and many dangers that we encounter on our journey to authenticity and productivity. Social media provide unprecedented opportunities for connecting, but that doesn't mean that they should be used promiscuously. It's important to use them efficiently to build a lasting, rather than superficial, network, one that is about quality, not just quantity.

Although it's not recognized as a medical condition, Internet addiction has become so prevalent that treatment centers and twelve-step programs are now available to help treat it. At a recent conference where I spoke, I asked audience members to raise their hands if they checked their email at least a hundred times a day. Seventy-five percent of attendees' hands popped up. If you raised your hand, you too may need to reduce your Internet usage to stay at maximum productivity.

Joe Marchese, an SVP at Fuse Networks, provided an example of how he manages emails to improve his positive productivity. Mr. Marchese travels extensively and creates an Outlook folder, by city, of emails that say, "I'll let you know when I'm in town." Two days prior to his arrival to a city, Joe looks at all of the emails in a folder and sends out a group invitation to all friends and associates for dinner or drinks. He added, "It's a very efficient way of staying in touch." Joe is using both online and offline skills to network in a very collaborative and efficient way. Several other tips for email management include:

- Follow a "delete, delegate, or respond" philosophy.
- Use a bounce back if you're on deadline or will not be checking emails, and include contacts for further information.
- Use one email account for purchases and online accounts and a second address for purely business dialogue.
- Unsubscribe to emails if they are not useful.
- Include links to your social media addresses in your email signature.

I myself have added my name to the National Do Not Mail List so I do not waste time looking at catalogs of clothing or unneeded housing accessories. Taking advantage of cloud-based storage systems and backing-up programs and moving toward a paperless office can also save time and potential headaches. Develop a system to organize and track your online files and clean up your desktop monthly. Another great productivity tip is using automatic bill payment systems and an online tool such as Mint to keep track of your budget and finances.

If your wallet is organized but your closet isn't, you may want to do a closet clean-out day. Take all shoes needing repair in to have it done and bag items you haven't worn for more than a year to give to Goodwill or the Salvation Army. Actions such as these will keep you organized so your time is maximized and spent on activities that have a greater return than procrastinating, organizing your home, or running errands.

Another way to avoid time wasters is to consider your values and goals prior to scheduling meetings and calls or saying yes to events. One tip is to always say, "I will get back to you," prior to committing to a meeting. Give yourself the opportunity to review your calendar, purpose, and goals. You may also wish to organize your calendar in a consistent fashion. For example, do calls in the morning and meetings at the end of the day, and dedicate the bulk of the day to thinking and work. If you have the luxury to make your own schedule, don't overschedule, to avoid crossing over from productivity into frenzy. In a generic sense, this means scheduling daily, weekly, and monthly networking activities that align with your goals but don't undercut your health or waste your valuable time.

For example, I received a coffee request via Twitter from a woman named Susan McPherson. I took a quick look at her Twitter bio, at @susanmcp1, and it was easy to see we had common interests. Even though social media bios are character-limited, they reveal a lot of information. For example, Susan's bio could put her into a community category of cause marketers. Another person's bio could put him or her into a category of CEOs, tech lovers, or mommy bloggers. This new data and information can be viewed to make sure you are connecting with people who share your interests. Eventually, when I was in New York City, I invited Susan to join a gathering of women I had assembled and a new friendship was formed.

Don't be afraid to say no to a meeting request. Recently, I received a very poorly written, typo-laden email from a filmmaker who wanted to send me her creative reel. Because I'm not active in the film industry, it did not make sense for me to accept the reel or schedule a meeting. It may feel awkward to say no, but a justified no is more thoughtful than an inefficient, time-wasting yes.

Be Efficient: Mix Business with Pleasure

Another effective way to maximize your positive productivity is to overlap your passions and purpose with your business and personal goals whenever possible. For example, can you host a business discussion while taking a walk? Can you share a ride with a coworker to be green and get work accomplished at the same time? Can you gather work associates at a benefit to support a charity that you're passionate about and also strengthen your work bonds? Think about potential overlaps. Be creative, and you may find that an approach of mixing business with pleasure brings a fresh perspective to some of your current routines or relationships. Or mix it up, but make sure your ideas suit all of the participants in your party and that you're not being self-serving. Your goal is to be efficient and create stronger networking bonds without alienating your friends or contacts.

Exercise 3: Do a time-waster audit.

If you're going to practice positive productivity, cut out your time wasters and move toward greater productivity. Time is the only resource we have that is nonrenewable. Once it's gone, you can't get it back. So take an inventory. Look at your average day, and see where you waste time. Several areas to review:

1. Commuting
2. Internet surfing/television viewing
3. Chatting/gossiping
4. Your morning routine
5. Unproductive thinking

One suggestion is to track your time over the course of a day or a week to see how you use it. There are several free applications and some with a monthly fee that are available online that can be used to track your time. Or do it the old-fashioned way on a notepad. Toss a yellow pad into your messenger bag or purse and track your time spent on various activities in half-hour increments. Are you overorganizing your house when you should be working? Are you texting when you should be thinking? Make a commitment to put your time, your relationships, personal finance, and health first.

Tune-up Tip: Discover what inspires you.

If you are feeling unproductive or looking for inspiration, I recommend listening to music or exercising. Take time out to relax and focus your thinking on your purpose. Helping others is also a good way to gain perspective. What imagery can you keep in your mind? What music can you play to help you move into greater productivity?

Now that you've completed chapters 1 to 3 of *Your Network Is Your Net Worth*, you are on your way to improving your networking skills. Remember, the key to positive productivity includes looking at obstacles and opportunities in small parts, doing a time-waster audit, mixing business with pleasure (when appropriate), and creating a purpose plan.

Chapter 3: Summary

Step 3: Create a mind-set of positive productivity.

Exercise 1. Create an action list or purpose plan.

Exercise 2. Conduct a collaboration review.

Exercise 3. Do a time-waster audit.

Tune-up Tip: Discover what inspires you.

Top Tips

1. Take small actions to solve larger problems or find opportunities.
2. Maximize pivot points.
3. Remember that collaboration aids success.
4. Streamline your time spent on the Internet.
5. Unsubscribe to emails as much as possible.
6. Do mix business with pleasure.
7. Listen to music or exercise for inspiration.

4

Give Give Get

Why It's the Real Networking Secret

A key to unlocking the hidden power of connections is helping others when you don't expect anything in return. It's not as easy as it sounds.

It's true; small actions can have a large impact. If you put giving back and helping others at the center of your networking and relationship building, you are likely to have more impactful and stronger relationships, among other benefits. By seeing networking as an opportunity to help people, I've discovered that these actions change me for the better and help me transition out of negative states of emotion. The phrase I've coined to help you remember this idea is "Give Give Get"; that is, put greater energy into giving than receiving. What you will find is that the giving will come back to you tenfold. A focus on giving can transform your emotional state, improve your relationships, build your happiness quotient, and teach you the importance of gratitude.

In this chapter, I'll share some approaches for giving to others in your personal and professional circles that can yield positive outcomes for the giver, the receiver, and other associates in your networks. We know that fostering happiness and well-being requires a sustained focus on behaviors that range from activism and mentoring to volunteering and financial giving and usually involve developing your spiritual and emotional depth. What I want to share in this chapter are the enormous possibilities that are latent in our everyday connections, in the thousands of professional and extended associations available to us. Through Give Give Get we can apply the principles of happiness and positive living in small moments and microexchanges or in larger actions, sometimes creating friendships and professional alliances and other times improving everyone's day for a while.

Step 4: Develop a Give Give Get attitude.

There are two exercises in Step 4. In Exercise 1, you will conduct a Give Give Get review. In Exercise 2, you'll review the value of mentoring.

The act of giving back can be as simple as making a donation or saying hello or as complicated as helping others overcome extreme adversity. I recall fondly a day when my daughter and I were heading to the local Safeway. The parking lot was a zoo of suburban moms with their Starbucks cups commandeering their Prii (the Toyota-approved plural of Prius) and SUVs into empty spots. A gem of a space, near the front of the lot, looked empty, but as cars turned into the space, a red shopping cart sat askew in the space with its front wheels hooked on the cement divider. As we walked past the spot, Rylee, my daughter, turned to me. "Mommy, should I move that shopping cart?" she asked. A smile grew across my face. "Sweetie, that's a great idea. You'll be helping the next person who tries to park."

I'm not sure who was positively impacted that day when Rylee moved the shopping cart, but it is probable that her small action helped someone. Perhaps it was a senior citizen shopping for produce? Or maybe a fender bender was avoided between a station wagon and the red cart? I do not know the outcome, but I do know that small actions make a difference. Jeff Pulver, a cofounder of Vonage and the creator of the 140 Characters Conference, posts daily inspirational quotes on his Facebook page. His posts range from "Don't let your past block your future" to "Don't be afraid to be you." They generate numerous "likes" and comments. His small online actions send positive messages to his large virtual community and may help someone right side a day that may have been going south. When I spoke to Jeff, he said, "The best gift you can give someone is believing in them. I hope my daily messages inspire others."

While conducting interviews for this book, I was surprised at the number of people who had early childhood memories of giving back or helping neighbors. One friend said, "I remember carrying chairs up from the basement and putting the extra leaves into the table and handing out coffee to friends of my parents who were involved with the school." Another recalled "stuffing envelopes and sending faxes to help spread the word about local politicians."

I fondly recall the day Rylee decided she wanted to set up her first lemonade stand. "How about in front of the guide dogs?" she asked. So I called the group that trains service animals, which is located near our house, and asked, "Can my daughter do a lemonade stand in front of your facility and donate the funds to your group?" "Of course, we have our annual puppy fair coming up. Do you want a booth?" said the voice on the other end of the line.

When the day arrived, Rylee made a large LEMONADE FOR PUPPIES sign, and we filled our car with Costco-sized containers of lemonade mix, at least a hundred lemons, tons of ice, and three large plastic jugs that looked as though they should have been on the sideline of a high school football game. As we turned the corner toward the facility, cars were lined up and down the road, and crowds of people were entering the campus. The faces of the people were covered with bliss, as if they were heading to a free concert in Golden Gate Park, not a puppy exhibit and dog fair. We set up Rylee's station and served drinks for hours and hours. Many folks took Rylee's sign literally and thought we were peddling lemonade for dogs. The day took effort, but it had a triple bottom line: Rylee helped others, she raised over $500 for Guide Dogs for the Blind, and the eventgoers didn't go thirsty.

Another small Give Give Get we do is that we share our baked goods with our neighbors. I'm a fan of the Barefoot Contessa's *Barefoot Contessa at Home* cookbook and have mastered the coconut cake recipe, but we've never been able to finish an entire cake, let alone the dozens of cookies we bake. You'll often see us out and about handing out paper plates filled with hot muffins or cookies. The payback is hard to describe. We get waves from neighbors raking their leaves, bags of homegrown apples set on our doorstep, and I'm not sure who does it, but my garbage cans are always put away after pickup day when I'm traveling. These small things may seem insignificant, but each action brings a community or network together action by action and step by step.

Exercise 1: Do a Give Give Get review.

Take out your journal and write down some of the ways you Give Give Get. Include both small actions and big efforts. Do any of your actions reinforce your passions and purpose? If not, consider finding organizations, efforts, or people you may want to help to reinforce your passions. To increase your Give Give efforts, ask yourself these five questions:

1. Who can I help in my community?
2. How can I help in my workplace?

3. Do I want to support any nonprofits?
4. What can I do each day to make a difference?
5. What type of Give Give actions will support my passions and purpose?

The Greatest Joy: Creating Activists

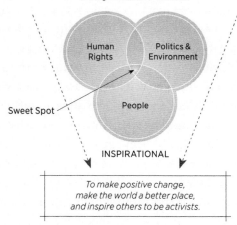

Amy Rao's Funnel

Human Rights

Politics & Environment

Sweet Spot

People

INSPIRATIONAL

To make positive change, make the world a better place, and inspire others to be activists.

Amy Rao, the CEO of Integrated Archive Systems, who told me that she detasseled corn for nine summers and once worked in a factory making plastic toilet seat screws, said, "The more you give, the more you get. I feel incredibly privileged, beyond privileged. I never dreamed I would have the life I have. I grew up on the lower end of the middle class. My dad had a shoe store, and in a good year he made about $20,000. When finances were tight, my mom would drag my two sisters and me to the store so we could take advantage of 'limit two sales': each of us would grab two cartons of milk, and we'd bring them home and freeze them. Did you know you can freeze milk?" She smiled. "That said, every year my dad would choose one or two families in the community that had kids and couldn't afford shoes. He'd have them come into the store, and he'd measure their feet and we'd take them the shoes on Christmas Eve. You sort of never forget where you came from. I now give away as much as I can."

Ms. Rao supports numerous causes via donations, service, and board affiliations. "When my adorable daughter, Ahna, went to kindergarten, I started getting involved in politics because I realized the public schools were facing tough times, and they were largely funded by the state. I figured out that who was in charge would impact my child and the education she gets. That's when I wrote my first check to help Gray Davis get elected, as he had a great stance on schools." In Ms. Rao's case, her giving started locally, but she expanded it by turning her focus to national politics, the environment, human rights issues, and the arts. "Now Human Rights Watch is my basis for everything. I focus on it all the time, talk about it, and bring more and more people to it. It's an incredible bond for a network when you share such a purpose with people—you'll do anything for them. Good people tend to fall onto the same list and share the same passions," she added. "You always need to respect others and put yourself in someone else's shoes and not judge. We may come to things with a different lens, but the bottom line is, how do we make the world a better place?"

Ms. Rao feels that giving back and helping are a key to happiness. "I remember being at a friend's funeral and a mutual acquaintance said, 'She was always there for me, whenever I needed her, she would do anything for me.' That's how I'd like to be remembered too. If I leave the world with nothing but having created five activists [her children] and know that they care about things bigger than themselves, that's where joy comes from." She smiled. "I may push too hard; I have to remember that at nineteen I was working at Kentucky Fried Chicken and going to college. I didn't know what my passion was. My kids will come into it in their own way. I want them to be citizens of their community and of their world." Ms. Rao had a similar viewpoint about her sixty-plus-person team at the office: "The greatest joy isn't when they bring in the big elephant; what I love is seeing when one of them gives back. If they are giving a hundred dollars or a thousand dollars or a day of time, that is all I care about. What are you giving back? That's what defines us."

Tune-up Tip: Remember GRAPES.

Because my belief is that our net worth is based on more than assets and liabilities, I've coined the acronym GRAPES to guide your networking and net-worth-building efforts. Remember GRAPES, and you will stay on track:

G: Give Give Get

R: Relationship-focused

A: Authentic

P: Purpose-driven

E: Earnings

S: Success

The Power of a Dream: The Epicenter of What's Important

Diana Barnett, a self-taught photographer in Manhattan, also lives a Give Give Get mind-set: "I had decided to leave my career as a chef. Without a full-time job, I was in an in-between place that can be terrifying or exhilarating. The ground beneath your feet is gone, and you're meant to leap. Helping others with my

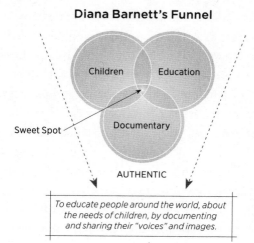

Diana Barnett's Funnel

Children
Education
Documentary
Sweet Spot
AUTHENTIC

To educate people around the world, about the needs of children, by documenting and sharing their "voices" and images.

photography couldn't have been a better leap." She told me that at the time she kept having a dream after seeing images of the 1999 earthquake in Turkey. "I kept waking up thinking about the children and decided I wanted to go photograph the kids and give them a face." Diana decided to research and network, and she determined that if within three weeks her plans came together it would be a sign that she was meant to go. She called and emailed friends, and before she knew it, she had a translator and a driver arranged. Next, she contacted several charitable organizations and offered to donate photographs to help raise funds and awareness of the postearthquake conditions. Then she jumped on a plane. "I couldn't believe how fearless I was. When I arrived, it was late, and we drove from Istanbul to the epicenter. I couldn't believe it. We were driving through devastation. It was dusty, and the buildings were shredded to pieces. It was almost hard to imagine, like we were on a movie set. It changed my life forever." Ms. Barnett said that they drove to a tented village. "We entered a tent, and it was full of these amazing women cooking food, and there was a fresh fig tree outside. Here they were living and doing the best they could, and there was a lot of positive energy."

The contrasts like these continued on her journeys. "I remember working with an organization in the northeast of Brazil in a city named Recife. They work with street children, and I met a young boy who had been abused, had cigarette burns, and was forced to beg by his family. He ran away and was taken in by a social worker," she said. "Even with his situation he expressed to me that he 'loved life.' I think there is some indescribable faith and belief that these children have. Maybe within their lives of simplicity they've somehow grown richer? Or perhaps they've found joy without a tremendous amount of stuff?"

Diana went on to document children for her Faces of Tomorrow project. She traveled to seven countries, funded by several charitable organizations. "I've learned so much and have so much gratitude for what they [my subjects] have given me and I've given them." She also gained more than expected when returning from a trip to Brazil. "Just before flying back home, I went to the island of Fernando de Noronha to swim with the wild dolphins. I was so happy, but I was running late to catch my flight. I looked like Linus [from the *Peanuts* comic strip] and had cameras hanging around my neck. I sat next to this man named Billy and asked if he could translate a newspaper story about a school shooting." The two chatted for nine hours straight. "We ended up spending the week together in Manhattan, and now it's twelve years later and we've been married for seven years. Giving back has given me so much lightness and joy. When we give, we learn and grow and are much happier."

Tune-up Tip: Practice a random daily give.

Ms. Barnett's favorite random give is swiping her subway card for someone with no rides left on his or her card. What random give can you practice, from saying hello on a hiking trail to leaving your recycling out for a person collecting cans? Little actions add up. Give a random gift, and see what happens.

Don't Expect Anything in Return: High Spirits

Another important aspect of living a Give Give Get mind-set is not expecting anything in return for your efforts or actions. Carter Reum, a cofounder with his brother of VeeV Spirits, says that he likes to build a rapport before asking for anything in return. Mr. Reum illustrated this with a story about how he ended up putting his early-stage liquor product aboard Virgin America planes: "I went to college with someone who works at Virgin Management. He called and asked if I could help find Sir Richard a venue for his book launch. I said yes and offered to sponsor cocktails too." Mr. Reum ended up starting a friendship with an employee from Virgin whom he met at the event. After they had a strong dialogue established, he asked for an introduction to the airline, which is how we met by phone. Shortly thereafter, partially because I could tell that the Reum brothers were living their purpose and also because I knew our fliers would love the product, I did recommend that VeeV be served on board flights. The company now sells more than a 100,000 units a year on the airline.

Also important, many of the core values of VeeV aligned with the DNA of Virgin America. The duo had created a hip, design-oriented company with sustainability ingrained into everything they do. The Reum brothers were giving but ended up getting in return.

Don't expect anything in return; this important point is central to values-based networking. It's a concept that you should apply to your offline, online, and social media strategies. It's also important to be authentic in your approach. For example, if you volunteer to support an arts organization, do it because you're passionate about the arts, not solely as a way to meet potential dates.

The same philosophy applies to social media: use it to further your values and goals, but do not expect a retweet for every tweet. In the world of social media, the rules and etiquette of giving and compensation are still in the early stages of evolution. The law is even further behind. For example, if someone continuously direct messages you on Twitter and asks you to tweet messages, it may be annoying, and you're likely to unfollow the person, but it is certainly not illegal. We don't have rules akin to the established principle of our legal system called the "officious intermeddler." Its premise is that you cannot expect payment for services provided if there was no prior agreement. For example, if you go on vacation and someone decides to wash your car, that person cannot bill you without prior agreement. Common sense, right? Unfortunately, this often *isn't* true in the networking and social media worlds, where people often give only to extract a specific get. I recall when a contact emailed and asked me to make a very large request on his behalf. That ask would have been fine, but without my prior agreement he had already prewritten a note, to be sent under my name, with the suggested ask. I remember sitting at my desk, perplexed and a bit put off by the request.

To counter this, I advocate that you should follow a Give Give Get philosophy. Do not expect follow-up actions from others based on your networking actions, social media posts and interactions. Your networking and social media efforts should be based on your desire to connect with people, share content, give insights, and live your purpose. "Social giving," not "social getting," should be the heart and core of your intentions. Give. Then give again. You'll see that what you get is much greater.

Since the Reum brothers launched VeeV, their business has skyrocketed, in part because the duo lives a Give Give Get philosophy. The Reum brothers now give 1 percent of their profits to environmental causes, including the Sustainable Açai Project to support local farmers in Brazil, and they hired a local women's co-op in the region to make more than 100,000 bracelets out of açai seeds per year. Because of their commitment to sustainability, the duo chose a distillery in Idaho that runs on wind power, they put bamboo floors in their office, and they use recycled packaging for their product. "I knew our values were strong when a natural beverage company offered us a vending machine and our office manager asked if it was Energy Star efficient," said Mr. Reum.

Not surprisingly, when I asked Mr. Reum for an interview, he gave me an hour of his time with less than a day's notice. It's certainly a plus when business relationships morph into friendships. Because the Reum brothers' values are clear and well defined, it's easy for contacts and companies to connect with them if their values are in sync. There's no gray area or confusion about the Reum brothers' passions or purpose.

The Power of Mentoring: From Simba to Sugar Packets

Another Give Give Get practice that can produce tremendous results is the act of mentoring. In the old model of networking, mentoring was a way to solve your problems and get what you wanted. In the new model, mentoring is a two-way street, with mentors often citing a greater emotional return than the perceived value of their donated time and effort. Mentoring is collaborating, both informally and formally, and helping others to learn so they can uncover their passions and true potential. Recently, Rob Minkoff, the director of *Stuart Little*, *The Forbidden Kingdom*, and numerous other films, visited a Los Angeles high school classroom to share the story of his life in the business. After talking about the ups and downs of his career and the importance of passion and commitment, he turned to the blackboard and drew a figure there. When he turned back to the class with a smile as wide as Texas, he revealed an image of Simba and noted, "And because of commitment and passion, I directed *The Lion King*." The classroom of students went wild with a roar of applause.

Over the phone, Mr. Minkoff shared why mentoring is so important to him: "When I was eighteen, I had just started at Cal Arts, and our class went to see a tribute to Mel Blanc, who was the voice of Bugs Bunny, Porky Pig, and a bunch of other characters." At the screening, one of Mr. Minkoff's classmates struck up a conversation with Chuck Jones, a director who had worked extensively with Mr. Blanc and created more than three hundred animated films. Mr. Jones graciously offered to share his story with Mr. Minkoff's classmate and several of his friends at his home studio at a future date. "Chuck ultimately became my most important mentor. He had an incredible career and never lost his wonder and enthusiasm for art. His inquisitive nature kept him young, and he was extremely gifted in art, painting, drawing, and filmmaking."

According to Mr. Minkoff, Mr. Jones's estate has several galleries that exhibit his work, and many important collectors have purchased his art. "Chuck used to host a weekend gathering every year with his collectors," said Mr. Minkoff. "When he passed, his daughter, Linda, asked me to fill in for him, in his memory." The morning of the event, Rob, who lives in Los Angeles, had assumed that the event was in Corona del Mar, where Mr. Jones resided. "I looked at the invitation and was shocked to see it was in San Diego. I panicked. There was no way I could get there in time. I'd be at least an hour or two late." Rob called a business associate who had a plane. "John, I'm going to ask you the biggest favor I've ever asked. I need you to fly me to San Diego right now." He explained the situation, and within five minutes his friend said, "Meet me at the airport." The two flew to San Diego; a car was waiting, and Rob sped off to the event. "I walked in, was only several minutes late. It was an honor and privilege to know him. Chuck changed my life."

Another example of the power of mentorship is the story of sixteen-year-old Hayley Hoverter, who invented a product called Sweet (dis)Solve, which *Forbes* later called "World's First Soluble Sugar Packets." She tracks her success back to the efforts of one person, Brent Freeman, the CEO of Roozt, who in 2011 taught a class on social entrepreneurship to a group of California high school students. During and after the class, Hayley came up with the product idea, secured investors, was invited to Starbucks to discuss her product, won a national youth entrepreneur fair, and was even invited to the White House.

Because of Brent, Hayley has been introduced to "more people than I can count"—from lawyers to newspaper writers to bloggers to social activists and especially fellow entrepreneurs. When I asked Brent about Hayley's success, he said, "Hayley is an example of what can happen when we believe in people, value them, and give back to our business communities." He added, "I saw her transform from the shyest student in the class to an experienced business leader—and she's only seventeen!"

Kim Diamond, a real estate consultant, remarked, "It's funny how you touch people and don't even know it. I met a young architect who needed reassurance that it was okay to be herself and to network and ask people for coffee. I guess I gave her confidence unknowingly when we became friends." She continued, "A couple of years later, I ran into her in LA at a conference. She had just had a baby and was back out there, and she came up to me and tears welled up in her eyes. She shared how I had really touched her. It was so sweet. For all the people that have helped me, I try as much as I can to help others."

To show the power of mentoring, following is a partial email that was sent to Nancy Gale, the director of the entrepreneurial program In True Fashion, by a mentee in one of her classes:

When I woke up this morning I felt uninspired and unmotivated to go to school. Not only that, I have been depressed, insecure and feeling like I can't move on in life. The lesson about networking today really opened my eyes. I have always been in a shell and afraid to try new things, but this lesson is getting me to change my mind. I hope that I can learn to network and have great opportunities so that I can be successful and smile all the time like you do. Thank you and see you next week!

Exercise 2: Try mentoring for growth and giving.

Take out your journal and write down the names of meaningful mentors in your life. Consider their impact on your professional or personal development. If you're seeking advice, ask a respected professional to coffee for advice, or look for a professional mentoring group (e.g., Step Up Women's Network). If you have advice or mentoring to give, look for a group to support (e.g., Big Brothers Big Sisters) or offer to mentor someone at the office or in your network.

Making Sense of Things: Helping Others Educate the Masses

Part of networking is always being up for adventures that create opportunities to meet new people. Prior to my departure from Virgin America, I was invited to attend an America's Cup preliminary match in Cascais, Portugal. To go or not to go, that was the question. As it happened, I knew the CEO of an airline that flew into Portugal. I had spoken several times at his airline's events and had already agreed to fly to Germany in the future, at no charge, to present a case history on social media to his customers. I didn't expect anything in return for helping my airline CEO friend, but since we had an existing friendship and business relationship, I asked if he'd allow me to fly nonrevenue (for free if there was an empty seat) to Portugal. "No problem, we'll get you the seat," he said. So I called a friend who was already in Europe, and off to Portugal I flew.

If jetting off to Portugal sounds too good to be true, remember that points from miles and credit card programs add up quickly. Save your frequent-flier miles and consolidate them on a site such as Points.com for special opportunities or Give Give Get adventures.

On that quick trip we motored next to the America's Cup race boats in the day and attended parties, went dancing, and sang karaoke at night. I came home after several days of laughter with some great photos and several new connections. One of the people I met on the trip was Mark Buell, the chair of the San Francisco America's Cup Organizing Committee. I was standing next to Mark at an evening concert when I overheard him giving advice to a local woman who wanted to get into social work. He said, "You might want to volunteer first to make sure you like the work." What struck me was that as other people were bellying up to the bar, Mark was giving advice to a woman who was working at the event.

I met with Mark several months later to chat about networking and giving. "I guess I could just fly-fish or golf all day, but being a civic leader and the social interaction it entails helps me make sense of it all," he told me. He has had a long list of job titles at this point in his life and appeared to like the title "Mr. President" of the San Francisco Recreation and Park Commission the best. "I get paid ninety-seven dollars a month for one job, zero for another and zero for another. It's not about money, as I'm somewhat retired. I just like climbing bigger mountains and find the work empowering." He added, "I didn't know I had the juice for the America's Cup position, but I used to get up in the middle of the night to watch the races. I am passionate about San Francisco and sailing and knew I'd always wonder what would have happened if I said no to the opportunity."

Mr. Buell tries to help individuals when he can. The day I met him for lunch, he had spent the morning with a woman who had been with the Red Cross for ten years and had recently lost her job due to cutbacks. "My heart goes out to people in these situations. I can't promise anything but will try to connect people with new opportunities when possible," he told me.

Lynn Hirshfield also has a focus on giving back and works as a senior vice president of publishing at Participant Media. She is also an author and a strong values-based networker. She described the film company's mode: "We follow a triple-bottom-line policy: our projects have to be profitable, produced in a sustainable fashion, and they need to move the needle on social change." Ms. Hirshfield described herself as a guinea pig to the masses: "If I don't know about the issue, then others should be educated about it too."

Hirshfield's personality helped seal the deal when she met with a very large team of filmmakers, with Al Gore joining via a video conference call, to talk about the marketing of the award-winning film *An Inconvenient Truth* back in 2005. "They all kept talking about carbon footprints, and at the end of the meeting I asked where I could get a pair. I thought they were those little odor-eater mats that you put in your shoes," she said with a smile.

When the carbon-footprint mystery was revealed, Lynn realized she needed and wanted to get behind the film in a "big way." She told me that her desire to do good and connect people is "like having Tourette's syndrome and is unconscious, not premeditated. I feel I have an obligation to help good people and spread the word about causes." When I mentioned to a mutual friend that I had met Lynn, the friend said, "She could close five deals in the Sahara Desert, she knows everyone, and people love working with her." It's easy to see that Ms. Hirshfield's authentic approach and strong sense of values have helped her build a rich and socially motivated network.

I'll finish this chapter with a simple tip: keep a Give Give Get mentality by working to remember the simple phrase "How can I help?" At a recent dinner the entrepreneurial coach Ali Brown graciously offered to help several of us at the table. She was also the first to shake hands with and introduce herself to the restaurant owner. She connected not only with her tablemates but also with the restaurant team. She was a true networker in action but was giving to others in a very simple way, by acknowledging them and offering help. Her offer was sincere and thoughtful and was just four simple words: "How can I help?"

Chapter 4: Summary

Step 4: Develop a Give Give Get attitude.

Exercise 1. Do a Give Give Get review.

Tune-up Tip: Remember GRAPES.

Tune-up Tip: Practice a random daily give.

Exercise 2. Try mentoring for growth and giving.

Top Tips

1. Don't expect anything in return.
2. Teach Give Give Get to others.
3. Incorporate social responsibility into corporate efforts.
4. Mentor to yield unexpected returns.
5. Use the phrase "How can I help?"

5

Shake It Up

Change Your Routine to Unlock New Growth

Shaking up your routine and exploring new opportunities can change your life. Sometimes change is by choice and sometimes it is due to external circumstances. Regardless of where it comes from, it always has the potential to bring positive growth and learning.

We've all been there, complacent in our comfort zone. I lived in Manhattan for more than seven years, and on any given day I typically went to the same deli, the same coffee shop, and the same ATM and walked the same route to my office. What would have happened if I had changed my routine? How would my life be different? What if I had dropped Starbucks and only gone to independent coffee shops? What would have happened if I had started taking tennis lessons on the roof of the club up the West Side Highway?

In this chapter, we're going to talk about shaking it up and the impact changing your routine can have on your transformational networking efforts.

Sometimes change is self-motivated, and sometimes it is a result of outside influences. It's not always easy to predict, but when you anchor your core values and practice positive productivity, you will more successfully navigate the highs and lows of your journey. In this chapter, we will look at ways you can proactively shake it up by changing your routine, trying events designed to meet new people, embracing unemployment (if it happens), and getting outside of your comfort zone.

Step 5: Commit to shaking it up.

For Step 5, you will complete two exercises. The first is to define three Shake It Up activities. The second is to organize a Shake It Up activity with friends.

Change Your Routine: Getting into the Swing

A change of a routine can be as small as taking a new route to work or as large as taking up a new hobby or moving to a new city. In January 2001, filled with nervousness, trepidation, and uncertainty, Kim Diamond walked up the stairs at the Metronome Dance Center in San Francisco and started taking dance classes. Several years earlier, an in-house creative team at The Gap had created an advertisement called "Khaki Swing" that was hailed as propelling swing music back into the mainstream and sparking a new generation of dancers. The spot, directed by the famed photographer Matthew Rolston, has over 800,000 views on YouTube. One of the people who saw the ad was Ms. Diamond. With the images in the back of her mind, she attended a work function that included dancing and decided that her New Year's resolution would be to take dance classes. "I didn't know what to wear, who would show up, or what would happen, but I knew I loved dancing as a kid," she said. "What happened was incredible. Dancing reignited a feeling of passion, excitement, and spontaneity in me. No other thing gave me that same feeling."

Kim explained that she had been relatively new to the San Francisco area and that a long-term relationship had just ended. "I met so many new friends, but more important, I learned to be in the moment. In my professional life I was always a leader and in control. But in social dancing I had to learn how to trust and be a follower and not the lead." She added that the experience had opened her heart. "I felt like I was falling in love. One friend that I made, named Julie, still teases me because I went to the first dance class wearing big heavy loafers. We still laugh because I was the loudest dancer in the room."

Kim's passion for dance demonstrates how tapping into new or long-neglected activities can bring joy and provide powerful, authentic opportunities for making new connections. Solid, long-lasting networks are built through defining common interests and places where we can relate to others and feel a sense of belonging. In Kim's case, her feelings of "love" can be attributed to finding a joyful activity and place where she "belonged." The natural boost we get during dancing and physical movement was probably a big factor, as exercise has been shown to release serotonin, dopamine, and other natural brain chemicals that generate a sense of well-being. Think of this as you are considering new adventures, routines, or experiences.

Go to Events Designed to Meet Others: Finding Love at Madame X

Another way to shake it up is to go to events and programs specifically designed for meeting new people. From meet-ups, speed dating, and speed networking to good old-fashioned civic clubs, you might be surprised what you can learn about yourself and the types of people you can meet. If you're worried about the potential time commitment, ask a friend to join you so you'll be positively productive.

For example, several years ago, Marjorie Spitz, a marketing consultant, decided to give speed dating a try. "I wanted to jump-start my romantic life, as things were a bit staid. I'm very social, so speed dating wasn't a chore; it was like going to a party," she explained. One evening, after being home for an extended period following foot surgery, Ms. Spitz and a girlfriend planned an evening in lower Manhattan. The duo started the night at a hip restaurant in SoHo and then headed to a speed-dating event at Madame X, a bar on West Houston Street, which is described on its website as "a plush, bordello-style lounge with comfortable couches, sexy red lighting, great cocktails and no attitude." Ms. Spitz noted, "I didn't like online dating, as I felt so much rejection and a lot of people were not truthful, and blind dates always felt like job interviews. But with speed dating you get to see if there's energy, you can judge someone's personality, and it doesn't feel unnatural. The six minutes may seem very, very long or very short." From speed dating, Marjorie met a "nice Jewish correction officer, the owner of a bike messenger service, and lots of people I would have never met," and she exchanged pleasantries with Bob, the man who would become her husband. "He had a nice smile, was very positive, and frankly was much nicer than the guys I was used to dating. I almost didn't pick him, as I'm usually attracted to 'bad boys' and people who are unavailable."

Luckily for the now-happy duo, several months prior to the outing Marjorie had started seeing a "love coach" who had helped her define and see what she really wanted and deserved in a relationship. "I made a list of the ten things I wanted and the five things I didn't want from a relationship. And when I thought about it, Bob had all the qualities on my list," she said.

"The universe posed an interesting challenge to me. You want this? Well, here it is; I'm going to give it to you, so what are you going to do with it?" Ms. Spitz described the process as "a bit scary, when someone is actually available and likes you." "We had our ups and downs, but I kept going, as I knew Bob was a quality person that I cared about and liked being with; ultimately things blossomed and turned into love, engagement, and marriage."

Exercise 1: Find three Shake It Up activities that support your passions.

Go online or look in your community paper for event listings, classes, or three other activities that you can do to shake it up and step closer to your passions. For example, if one of your passions is food, consider taking or teaching a cooking class or touring a local food market. Make a commitment to shake it up three ways in a month.

A New York Designer Becomes an Extra in *Sex in the City 2*

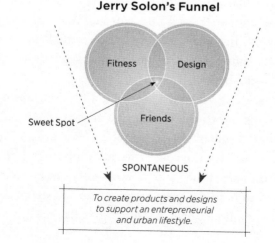

Jerry Solon's Funnel

Jerry Solon, a designer and entrepreneur who lives in New York City, shook it up and challenged himself when he responded to a random email he received looking for extras for the *Sex in the City 2* movie that was shot in 2009. At the time, Jerry was in Duluth, Minnesota, about to have dinner with his family when he saw the post. He was about to delete the message but instead responded and sent photos. Why not? His interest in acting was growing, and the opportunity worked with his schedule.

Within twenty minutes, he received a call from Grant Wilfley Casting; the contact said he'd been selected and he should be back in Manhattan in two days with a tuxedo in hand. Jerry jumped on a plane, headed back to the Big Apple, and borrowed a tux. As fate would have it, when his plane landed his left eye was swollen and sty-ridden. Worried and not sure if the sty was from stress or a bug bite, Jerry called friends and asked for their advice. "I bought eye drops and spent the next twenty-four hours alternating putting tea bags and a hard-boiled egg on my eye. I had a fear that I'd be the ugly duckling in the land of beauty, but I didn't want to take anything for granted," he said. He headed to the shoot at Steiner Studios in Brooklyn. "Extras were being herded like cattle into large tents, forms and paperwork were signed, and we moved into hair and makeup," he recalled. "Patricia Field, the stylist of all stylists, with flaming red hair, approved my outfit, and a makeup artist sent me to get rid of my five o'clock shadow.

"The next thing I know, a guy with a headset taps my shoulder and brings me to the soundstage that is filled with a wedding set, white bridges, swans, lagoons, and a stream." The crew selected Jerry to play the role of wedding photographer, and his two-day extra part turned into a two-week job. Humorously, he was directed to hold the prop camera over his sty-ridden eye. "I stood with the camera over my puffy eye, like an eye patch, and took fake photos of Liza Minnelli, Cynthia Nixon, Sarah Jessica Parker, and the rest of the cast.

"How odd that I was in Duluth, Minnesota, just two days earlier," he added. The shoot finally wrapped, Jerry's eye cleared up, and he was about to return the borrowed tuxedo to a friend when his phone rang. "Are you free tomorrow at five A.M.? We need some more extras in *Wall Street 2*. Bring the tuxedo," the casting agent said. For Mr. Solon, one email turned into several memorable experiences. Since that time, Jerry's been offered several other acting jobs and has been balancing his design and entrepreneurial career with acting gigs.

The Power of Underwear: Professional and Emotional ROI

Nicholas Graham, the founder of Joe Boxer, likes to shake up his routines constantly. "If things get too routine, I'm bored," he said. Depending on the day, you can find him working on projects in New York City, San Francisco, or London or even on the island of Borneo. One memorable time Mr. Graham pitched Sir Richard Branson the idea of the first transatlantic underwear fashion show. "I heard Virgin Atlantic was doing their first flight from London to San Francisco, and I found a way to get the idea to Sir Richard. I didn't know him at the time, but why not go for it?" he said. "Next thing I know, we've sold the idea and I'm on the inaugural flight with Sir Richard, several celebrities, and a plane full of excited passengers."

After several hours of craziness, Mr. Graham grabbed the intercom on the plane and announced, "There is a new immigration law: anyone entering the United States needs to have on clean underwear." Next, Sir Richard and Mr. Graham, "dressed in bad drag," pushed drink trolleys, full of boxer shorts, down the center aisles and tossed colorful undergarments to the passengers. Soon Mr. Graham made another announcement: "To change your underwear, put your tray table in the upright position, undo your seat belt, and put your pants around your ankles." He described a frenetic scene: "People were putting underwear over their clothes, and some passengers changed and didn't have any pants on." Then the fashion show turned conga line started. "Clarence Clemons, from Bruce Springsteen's band, was in the lead playing the saxophone. About fifty people were going up and down the aisles wearing underwear printed with happy faces, ants, or made from wild glow-in-the-dark colors—never in my life did I dream I would be at this moment. It was crazy, amazing, and fun."

Often, people like Mr. Graham reach a level of success or get there because they know when and how to shake it up. They lead the pack rather than follow it. They push boundaries and challenge norms without the need for instant gratification.

Mr. Graham added that he has pushed boundaries to make new friends. He shared how he met Eddie Izzard, the English stand-up comedian: "It was twelve or so years ago. I was lying in my bed watching *The Tonight Show*, and Eddie was on. I thought he was brilliant, and I just loved his work. Turns out I was going to New York the next day, and he was performing there. I went to the theater, found the owner, and asked for an introduction. When I met Eddie, I said, 'Comedy and underwear should go together,' and we ended up becoming friends." Graham continued, saying that making connections and meeting interesting people has more of "an emotional ROI than a financial one." I asked him how he approaches new friends. "Be confident in who you are, try making contact, and if someone is interesting, go meet them. You may not know where it will go, but it will probably make your life better and richer."

I've also met friends in unexpected places. Tom Stone, a

violinist I interviewed for this book, was my seatmate on a flight. I've also made connections that have changed my life at political fund-raisers, benefits, film festivals, dinner parties, on Twitter, through work collaborations, and more. Because time and schedules are precious, you need to shake it up in ways that fit with your goals, your life, and your current activities. Push your boundaries and challenge yourself; the people you meet could change your life.

Tune-up Tip: Shake it up by changing one small thing.

For example, try a different coffee shop. Take an earlier bus to work. Make time to photograph your favorite building, bridge, or piece of public art. Consider how small changes can make a big impact.

Unemployment and Setbacks: Pivot Points for Positive Growth

It's never an easy moment, but many successful people, including myself, have received a pink slip. Several years ago, I was the general manager of an advertising agency that decided to close the San Francisco office that I managed. It wasn't easy, but if it hadn't closed its doors, I would not be where I am today.

Dennis Crowley, the founder of Foursquare, includes in his Twitter bio that he "likes unemployment." When I asked him about that he explained, "I was laid off twice from two dot-com jobs, and I started Dodgeball.com as a thesis project. It was never supposed to turn into anything. It was a tool to make meeting up with friends easier. Then our project turned into a product. After some early success Google acquired Dodgeball.com but then shut it down in 2005. I started Foursquare to fill the void after that. It was pretty scrappy at first. We must have had thirty meetings to get funding. We had to hustle our way through it." He added, "I didn't know what else to do, as there weren't any companies I wanted to work for and I hated working for companies where there were 'haves' and 'have nots.'" Several years and a hundred new employees later, Dennis and his team have built an inspiring culture. "We all love working together. The key is acknowledging efforts and knowing it's a team. I keep everything very transparent." Like many successful networkers, Dennis is accessible on Twitter and has coffee meetings to give advice to people several times a week. He admitted, "I fell into this. It's easy to get stuck. When that happens it motivates you, and change really happens."

Stefanie Michaels, known as @adventuregirl on Twitter, shared her unemployment story with me. "Life and outside influences can throw you curveballs," she said. "In 2008, I was building my online brand, and three partnership offers were on my desk. A well-known search engine, an entertainment company, and an e-commerce site all wanted to cut deals with me. Several days later, the crash of 2008 began, and all three deals were pulled off the table. I was lying on the floor for a while, crying, and then realized I'd be okay one way or another and just rolled with it." Around the same time, Adventure Girl's husband had two surgeries for a brain tumor, his real estate business tanked, and the two almost lost their house. "We kept reducing the price of our house, but we couldn't sell it," she told me. "It's hard to have a Plan B, but I knew we'd figure it out. You need to be resilient and be good at ducking and covering. At the same time, I started noticing Twitter; it was a game changer. There's always pivoting. I focused on Twitter, blasted emails to my database and to all the press people in travel, and in three weeks I had 173,000 followers. I worked around the clock, but that was how I got my network back." While she was working to build up her platform, she had many sleepless nights, and her husband started referring to himself on Twitter as @Twidower.

With all the challenges on the table, Ms. Michaels still referred to the time as "funemployment." When I asked about the "fun" in "funemployment," she said, "I am back to my tech roots and doing what I love. When you set a goal to succeed, part of the fun is getting there." Today, Adventure Girl has more than 1.4 million followers on Twitter, and she is a travel personality and journalist.

Kim Diamond, the ballroom dancer and real estate executive, also faced a pivot point in September 2008. "As an executive with Pulte Homes for five years, working on a big project in the city of Orinda, California, near the BART station, I was provided with some protection," said Kim. "I didn't see it coming. My boss called me in, and I could tell it was incredibly hard for him to tell me I was being let go. He said the words *very* fast. He was a great guy and said all the right things, but I was in shock. I could feel tears welling up inside of me. I had never been let go before. It felt like someone was breaking up with me." She put on her sunglasses and was crying by the time she left the building. "I was incredibly sad and scared, but I felt a glimmer of hope inside of me and knew I would be okay," she said. She quickly turned to her network of business associates and contacts she had met through a group called the Urban Land Institute. "I was very honest with people and asked everyone I knew if I could take them to coffee to ask their opinion. People were very sensitive and my network was great, so everyone said yes." Since then, Ms. Diamond has transitioned from being an employee to the owner of her own real estate consulting firm. "I'm grateful now, but I don't think I would have left on my own. And I couldn't have done it without my network."

Exercise 2: Shake it up with friends.

Think about your passions and purpose and plan a group activity. Make sure you're taking steps toward your goals but not draining your bank account. Plan a potluck. Organize a group hike or try a new activity. Ask friends to bring a guest to meet connections with similar interests and passions.

As you can see, growth and positive change can happen when you least expect it. You have now completed part I of *Your Network Is Your Net Worth*. You are on your way to developing a transformational attitude and aptitude for your networking activities by creating an authentic foundation, anchoring your core values, practicing positive productivity, living in a Give Give Get mentality, and shaking it up. As you move into part II, the focus will shift from understanding your individual needs and actions to understanding the importance of building a values-based team to support your efforts.

Chapter 5: Summary

Step 5: Commit to shaking it up.

Exercise 1. Find three Shake It Up activities that support your passions.

Tune-up Tip: Shake it up by changing one small thing.

Exercise 2. Shake it up with friends.

Top Tips

1. Change your routine to unlock new growth.
2. Try events designed to meet others.
3. Reframe unemployment as "funemployment."
4. Lead the pack, don't follow.
5. Push boundaries and challenge the norms.
6. Be open to new conversations and connections.

Part II

Build a Values-Based Team

Problems can become opportunities when
the right people come together.
—ROBERT REDFORD

6

Three Degrees of Separation

Accelerate Your Connections with
Technology and Social Media

Technology has increased virtual intimacy and reduced the degree of separation between connections. New and old networking relationships may be just a tweet, a post, or an email away.

Toss out your old ideas: networking is no longer about climbing
a ladder to success with a Rolodex stuffed in a leather briefcase.
A different networking strategy is paying dividends in our global,
mobile economy: one that includes understanding your values,
having a positive attitude, and connecting with collaborators for
mutual inspiration, innovation, and support. In this part we will
explore how technology has changed how we connect, the importance of our core circle, the impact of power pockets, and the role
of hub players. From the macro perspective, part I is the *you* and
part II the *we* of transformational networking.

Technology is an obvious driver of this transformation. It has
accelerated networking, reduced the degree of separation between contacts, amplified our global playing field, and redefined
the job prospecting process. In this chapter, you'll see how social
media and online tools provide rich opportunities for learning
and help accelerate your efforts to make high-value connections.

Step 6: Accelerate your connections with technology.

You will find three exercises and two tune-up tips in this chapter. In Exercise 1, you will use online research to find communities and contacts. In Exercise 2, you'll make a list of people you would like to meet. Exercise 3 shows you how to make a job prospect list.

The New Standard of Communication

Can you imagine flipping a yellowed plastic accordion-style holder of photos from your wallet to show images to a friend? Or did you imagine years ago that new generations in the twenty-first century would text nonstop and look on email as being similarly antiquated? Technology is speeding up everyone's reaction time. One major accelerant: the distribution and use of smartphones. Our personal electronic devices (PEDs) have evolved from phone and email devices to video cameras, virtual wallets, online photo albums, and more. Kids talk about apps like I used to talk about Casey Kasem's *American Top 40* radio show; now watercooler conversations about the latest-version iPhone or tablet is the norm. As of the writing of this book, geeks are cool and Steve Jobs is a secular saint.

Technology and smartphones are being used around the globe to strengthen relationships. Skype calls and iPhone FaceTime help eliminate distance and keep connections alive. One contact whom I met via a friend on Facebook said, "For me, the most salient change during my twenty-three years in the workforce was when I started using a BlackBerry. This device changed how effective I could be and how I connect with people. It was a moment that everything changed. In an instant, the volume of my work leapt forward at an exponential rate. And people are now willing to accept electronic information with a lot more validity. The Internet has completely changed how we organize, connect, and mobilize different communities."

Technology also changed the fate of Henrik Werdelin and his wife, whom he met and dated long distance. They kept their long-distance relationship between Copenhagen and London thriving through Skype. After their conversations, they would leave the Skype line open so they could share the sounds of their environments and have a webcam window into their respective worlds. Henrik remarked, "We spent so many hours video-calling that we had a deeper understanding of each other." Technology was so important to the couple that Henrik's wife made an animated video for their wedding that ended with the phrase "The Werdelins, always together, always online."

Ultimately, the couple moved to New York City and Henrik taught his mother, in Denmark, to use Path, Skype, Facebook, and Twitter so she can be more involved in his daily life. His mother in turn wrote a book called *Mor på Nettet* (Mom on the Internet) to teach other families the benefits of using technology to stay connected. Soon after, she appeared on a morning talk show to discuss the book.

Being miles away didn't keep Robert Scoble, a blogger and technology evangelist, from attending a panel I was on in San Francisco. Mr. Scoble was in Half Moon Bay with a bunch of photographers he'd met on Google + when he connected virtually to the panel via iPhone FaceTime. From the beach, Mr. Scoble joined via the big screen and shared his viewpoints on online influence and a new product that was being launched. Technology also helped Shai Goldman, a director at Silicon Valley Bank, acclimate after he moved to Manhattan. I ran into Shai at a networking dinner where he told me, "I've been here ten months. But I feel completely at home, and I'm starting to see faces more than once." My past hypothesis was that it took at least two years to connect and feel grounded in a new environment. Shai and I agreed that technology has reduced the time a person needs to adapt to a new situation or surrounding. Social media can be used to organize impromptu meet-ups, flash mobs, and events, accelerating our potential to network, socialize, date, and rally. At any moment around the globe, millions of people are tweeting, posting, and pinning from homes, offices, trains, planes, automobiles, and even cruise ships.

Talking about cruise ships, last year I took my daughter on her dream vacation—a Disney cruise. Much to my surprise, many of the families on board had been chatting pretrip on a message board. Some had gone so far as to exchange berth numbers so they could deliver small gifts to each other's children to make the cruise extra special. The Disney cruise regulars even brought door hangers, or temporary mailboxes, for placement of the gifts. The Internet is not used only by Disney guests; a barista on the Disney boat keeps two Facebook pages, one for his personal connections and the other for people he meets on his adventures. This particular bar master, from San Juan, switches jobs every six months to make sure life is an adventure. "Next stop after Disney is Vegas," he told me. Whether you're going on a Disney cruise or to the Annual Sturgis Motorcycle Rally in South Dakota, finding subcommunities and people with niche interests has become easier.

However, social technology and email do not replace the real opportunity of friendship and professional collaboration. You need to give people you want to have serious relationships with as friends, romantic partners, or business colleagues real conversation and attention. Electronic tools only facilitate communication, therefore intensifying the effects of negative and destructive communication as well as positive, good-faith, bridge-building communication. My belief is that some of the factors that influence brand loyalty are also critical to networking loyalty, including trust, value, commitment, and transparency. So when building relationships both online and offline, consider the following:

- Do you follow through on your commitments?
- Can contacts trust you with information?
- Are you consistent with your relationships?
- Have you communicated that you value a given relationship?
- Is there a give and take within your relationships?

Tune-up Tip: Your network adds to your worth, so organize your contact information.

Find a system that works for you: enter contact information into your smartphone, use Outlook, connect on LinkedIn, or use a database software system. Keep notes on contacts such as birth dates, favorite foods, or passions.

Where to Draw the Line Online: Think Before You Post

Though online communications have reduced the degrees of separation between us, it's important to remember that social media raise a potentially tragic challenge (certainly for novices) in the area of privacy. To be a successful networker, you should be aware of privacy vulnerabilities and be able to navigate around the pitfalls. One flagrant example of this was dubbed "Weinergate" by the press when Democratic Congressman Anthony Weiner accidentally sent a sexually suggestive photo to a twenty-one-year-old woman on a public rather than private section of Twitter. Weiner later resigned from Congress. Even if you're not a politician or a celebrity, you should think twice before you tweet, post, or pin. A twenty-two-year-old who was offered a job tweeted, "Cisco just offered me a job! Now I have to weigh the utility of fatty paycheck against the daily commute to San Jose and hating the work." The candidate lost the job before she even started. The future career of a marine sergeant who criticized President Obama on Facebook is also in question, as the Marine Corps Administrative Separation Board recommended a less-than-honorable discharge, restricted the military man's access to computers, and stripped away his security clearance. He told the Associated Press, "I love the Marine Corps. I love my job. I'm having a hard time seeing how fifteen words on Facebook could have ruined my nine-year career."

A 2009 survey by CareerBuilder that was featured in an article in *The Atlantic* found that 45 percent of companies prescreen candidates on social media. Of those, 35 percent said they had found content that had caused them not to hire a candidate, with red flags cited including inappropriate photos, photos of excessive drinking, poor communication skills, excessive swearing, discriminatory comments, and confidential information posted about previous employers. So think before you post, especially when your emotions are high due to excitement, anger, or disappointment. Every image and comment you put online is building a future image for all of your present and future contacts, including employers, business associates, landlords, loan officers, and friends to see.

A CEO I know said, "I don't use social media, as I want to be invisible outside of the office." And a futurist said, "Privacy concerns are a big deal; soon you won't be able to do anything without your movements being tracked. In the future, people may pay for data-free experiences and confidentiality." At present, my view is that the benefits of social media and real-time connecting outweigh the negatives. However, it is extremely important to use the media appropriately and strategically. So when you're posting a party photo on Facebook, consider if you'd like it to show up on your timeline for an infinite period or if you'd like your next employer or business partner to see the image of you in a bikini or a Speedo with a cocktail in your hand.

Superficial to Superintimate Relationships

Similar to real-world relationships, your online relationships will range from superficial to superintimate. For example, you might be connected with contacts you've never met or you may be sharing dialogue with your closest family members or friends. It's important to understand and determine if you would like to use sites for different purposes or for nurturing different relationships. For example, I use Twitter to build my personal brand and to curate content that I find thought-provoking. And I have two Facebook pages—one for inner-circle relationships and one for business relationships. On my personal Facebook page you'll often see photographs of my hikes and family outings. However, it is not likely that I would share such posts on Twitter. There is also a site called Path that connects people with 150 of their closest and most intimate relationships. I also use Nextdoor to track conversations and dialogue with neighbors within a mile of my house. On this site neighbors post comments about lost pets and recommended babysitters, report recent crimes in the vicinity, and more. Google + (G+) and several sites do give you options to categorize relationships. For example, on G+ you can define a contact as a friend, a family member, an acquaintance, or a member of a subgroup that you self-define.

Regarding LinkedIn, one high-level executive recruiter said, "LinkedIn is by far the best professional networking tool. Even if you're not looking for work, you should have an updated profile."

Several recruiters I know do search LinkedIn and use it as a basis for finding potential candidates. I've also received inquiries about advising opportunities, partnerships, and more because of my professional listing.

If you're doing the searching, with LinkedIn you can find contacts by job title, and you can also see if you share common connections. For example, a past coworker who was entering the job market noticed that I knew the hiring manager at a technology start-up and emailed and asked me for a warm introduction. Serendipitously, the contact in question had recently contacted me to have coffee. Without being aggressive or crossing a line, I responded to the coffee request and asked her to look out for the résumé of my friend. Not surprisingly, the hiring manager didn't recall seeing the résumé but offered to review it and asked it to be resent. LinkedIn helped my contact secure an interview in less than three emails. LinkedIn also has functionality where you can search your Google contacts for known connections, has a box that recommends potential jobs of interest, recommends connections based on keywords in your profile, and with certain paid accounts you can see who has viewed your profile.

They Love You, You Love Them Back

If you want to build a relationship with a contact online, it's important to share, communicate, and connect in the same way that brand fans and companies nurture their relationships. Actions as simple as a retweet (RT) or mention in a #Follow Friday (#FF) list on Twitter, a "like" on Facebook or an endorsement on LinkedIn can signal your interest in connecting. Or you can have full conversations with connections of all levels with real-time dialogue and chats. When I was vice president of marketing at Virgin America we were the first airline to implement full-fleet

Wi-Fi at 35,000 feet. The service is now frequently used by fliers, and it allowed the author Peter Sims and me to have a Facebook chat between seats 15A and 19D when we ran into each other on a plane. Minutes later, others on the ground joined the conversation by liking and adding comments to our stream. One author engaged in our dialogue, John Serpa, sent me a message on LinkedIn: "Hello Porter, I was bantering on FB with you and Peter. I'll follow you on Twitter, too. Twitter is the best thing since smoothies." The virtual conversation with Peter gave me a new connection to John, and he invited me to his book signing.

Reduced Degrees of Separation

Because of technology, the number of degrees of separation between our contacts has reduced. The team at PeopleBrowsr, a company that has analyzed Twitter data from 2007 to the present, has a hypothesis that on a global level we're four degrees apart, on a community level (e.g., fitness lovers) we're three degrees apart, and on a niche level (e.g., love kite surfing) we're two degrees apart. New relationships may be just a tweet or an email away. Because we're in a data and analytics revolution, there are companies that can help you find communities of interest online.

So think about your purpose and passions. What types of people and communities are you interested in meeting? Try the next exercise and see what and who you can find to bring you one step closer to your purpose.

Exercise 1: Explore social media sites and use online research to find communities and connections.

Prior to this exercise, refer to chapter 2 and remember your purpose and personal mantra. Use them as a guide to filter your online community connections. For example, if you said you love fashion or food, look for communities or people with similar interests.

1. Explore Pinterest to find communities and people with similar interests.
2. Use StumbleUpon to curate articles, sites, and content.
3. Look for bloggers or digital influencers who write about your passions and follow them. Send them a tweet if you like their posts.
4. Follow people on Twitter who share your passions.

So the world has moved from the famous six degrees of separation, a concept made famous by playwright John Guare, to two, three, or four degrees of separation. At any given moment, anywhere in the world, you are likely to be somehow connected to those sitting near you in a room or on a plane or even passing you on a cobblestoned street in Europe. The world is one big interconnected web of relationships sewn loosely together via a broadband pipe, a LinkedIn connection, or a Pinterest page. And there are probably only a few degrees of separation between you and me.

Six Students Meet a Billionaire: Forty-five Life-Changing Minutes

One remarkable story that demonstrates how the world is getting smaller is the tale of how six high school students at a charter school in Los Angeles ended up securing a forty-five-minute meeting with Sir Richard Branson.

Several years ago, I met Nancy Gale (see chapter 1), a friend, entrepreneur, and activist, at an event. Nancy lives in Los Angeles and makes high-end leather handbags and teaches entrepreneurialism to underserved youths. She mentors a group of students at the Environmental Charter High School who were up for an award that included a potential visit from President Barack Obama if the school won a voting contest. Using their technical and creative skills, the students made personalized videos and sent them to key influencers who they thought could help them spread the word about the contest. One of the videos, addressed in the voice-over to Sir Richard Branson, landed in my email box.

Impressed by the video and the effort that the kids had put into the project, I forwarded the video to Sir Richard and asked if he'd vote for the school. First, I should tell you that I worked for Virgin America for four years, and there are more than 50,000 employees in Virgin-branded companies worldwide. I've met the amazing Sir Richard half a dozen times, but I don't think he'd recognize me on a street corner. Over the course of my time leading marketing at Virgin America, I presented him with research on types of airplane seats, showed him and several CEOs updates on our loyalty programs across all the Virgin airlines, and had a memorable meeting in Orange County, California, where we talked about a reality show called *Fly Girls* that I pushed through the Virgin system. So Sir Richard knows me, but I had never asked him for a favor. When I sent him the video, I never expected what followed.

Within twenty-four hours, Sir Richard called me on my cellular phone. It was the second call of my Virgin career that I received from him. The first was to confirm the address of a meeting location. The second was to tell me that he was in Los Angeles and could meet the schoolchildren that afternoon at 5 P.M. at the Sunset Marquis Hotel. That call, like the first one, shocked me. Never in a million years had I thought the kids would score a meeting with Sir Richard in less than twenty-four hours by sending him a video. I had been hoping for a tweet from @richardbranson, a virtual note via Ustream, or a Skype call. I'd never expected Sir Richard to rearrange his schedule to meet the group of high school students.

Looking back, I should have realized that this was exactly what he'd do. I never had a conversation with Sir Richard where he wasn't kind, humble, or thinking of the greater good. With all the crazy stunts, amazing parties, and people I've met, that moment will always be the highlight and most cherished memory of my time at Virgin America. I rang Nancy, and she gathered the students and drove them to the hotel. Many of them had never been out of their neighborhoods, let alone had a private meeting with a billionaire. Sir Richard spent forty-five minutes with the kids asking about their passions, the obstacles they might be facing, and why they wanted to be entrepreneurs. He changed the lives of six students and infused an entire school with a new sense of pride and passion. When business leaders heard that Sir Richard had met with the students, additional doors began to open. Soon the founder of a major skin care company, an early-stage Google executive, a film director, and many others visited Nancy's classroom and filled the room with words of encouragement and advice. To this day, when Nancy teaches the students she evokes the rhetorical question "What would Richard Branson say?" I'm sure they had no idea they were just three degrees away from Sir Richard Branson when they put their energy and creativity into their video request. I'm guessing that if they had asked their friends or anyone they knew if they could get a meeting with Sir Richard, the answer would have been "Never in a million years."

The lesson here is that the students did their homework on Sir Richard. They made a video that was specific and tailored to his interests, and they believed that anything was possible. It may be the innocence of youth, but a "can-do" attitude and a passion to make things happen are core ingredients in the recipe that makes one a successful networker.

Another example of how social media have changed real-time networking happened when two of my friends who are not connected attended the same event. One friend with the Twitter name @bradyhahn was an event speaker, and another with the Twitter handle @anjelikadeo was in the audience. During Brady's speech she mentioned my name, and as a result Anjelika knew I was connected to Brady and sent me a tweet. By copying my response back to both women, I encouraged them to meet and thus helped to bring together two like-minded professionals with similar interests. Prior to social networking, this chain of actions could have happened, but not instantly, while the event was still taking place. This type of real-time dialogue via social networking can be a great way to build your connections and network.

Anjelika followed through on her tweet and approached Brady after her presentation. The two connected initially because they both knew me, but after a brief conversation, they arranged a brunch date and started their own direct relationship. This type of Twitter connection is exactly how I ended up having Dr. Andy Baldwin, of ABC's *The Bachelor* fame, as my date to a Condé Nast magazines party in Los Angeles.

Several years ago, I received a Twitter message from Dr. Baldwin noting that we both knew a travel industry blogger named Johnny Jet, or @johnnyjet. Johnny has more than 30,000 Twitter followers, and Andy and I follow him or read his Twitter stream. One day Johnny posted a photo of me from a travel party, and Andy and I connected after he learned I worked for Virgin America. For six months, we had a virtual friendship solely via Twitter direct messages. Yes, that may seem odd, but we are living in a time when complete relationships can begin, evolve, and end via text messages.

For a couple of months, I didn't realize Andy had a résumé that included reality dating show fame. Andy's self-described Twitter bio said, "U.S. Navy doctor, fitness advocate, TV personality, Ironman tri-athlete, marathon runner and ardent supporter of military families." I missed the television personality notation, so imagine my surprise as I filled in that piece of our virtual communication puzzle.

We sent direct messages on Twitter about working out, travel, and his efforts to fight the problem of childhood obesity. Finally we decided to meet, and Andy drove to Los Angeles to be my escort to a party. I didn't get a red rose or find my bachelor, but I did make a friend and found a person with the similar interests of giving back and creating positive social change. Andy and I stay in touch via Twitter. I can count on one hand the number of times we've chatted on the phone, an indication that traditional modes of relationship building really have shifted. We help each other by retweeting (RT) or republishing our respective blog content, and our paths have crossed at several speaking events.

In addition, a CEO and former triathlon training partner of Andy noticed my connection to him on Twitter and asked me to have coffee to discuss marketing. Soon after, I joined the advisory board of his company and that relationship led to additional opportunities and conversations. This example reinforces that you cannot predict how connections will unfold. The examples of the kids meeting Sir Richard and my meeting Dr. Andy Baldwin show how quickly a new connection can impact your life. These stories demonstrate how important it is to be engaged and to ask questions, and the power of being open.

Because I'm a frequent flier, I often meet people on planes. With your purpose in mind, think about venues and locations that may provide opportunities to connect. Next time you're at the health club, a lecture, or a sporting event or even at the grocery store, try saying hello to or asking a question of a potential contact. You may end up one connection closer to your purpose.

Exercise 2: List three people you would like to meet.

In this exercise, write down three people you'd most like to meet. My list includes President Bill Clinton, Oprah Winfrey, and the writer Anne Lamott. In chapter 12, I'll tell you about my attempts to meet President Clinton, who is known as the master of networking. Keep this list, and in part III you'll make attempts to connect and meet these contacts.

You can also try posting networking questions to your Facebook friends, ask to be connected to contacts via LinkedIn, or ask for references of people interested in certain topics. Here's a story about how I ended up having lunch with the ambassador of Hungary.

Pretrip Planning: Find Friends, Not Just Restaurants

In 2011, I spoke about social media at a conference in Budapest, Hungary. About a week prior to the journey, I put up a quick post to my 1,110 Facebook friends: "Do any of you have connections or recommendations in Budapest?" Instantly, an email popped up from a friend: "I know the Ambassador to Hungary. She's in Budapest. I'll see if she'll have lunch with you."

To my surprise, within forty-eight hours, I had a lunch secured in Budapest with Ambassador Eleni Tsakopoulos Kounalakis. To add to the excitement, I had never met an actual ambassador, nor had I been to a U.S. Embassy. So after my very long transatlantic flight, I found my way, bleary-eyed, to my hotel, which was walking distance from the embassy. I grabbed a map, started snapping photos on my iPhone, walked across a bridge covered with gargoyles, and arrived outside the large stone building with an American flag flying over the foyer that crisp fall morning. At the gated entrance, I shared my identification, placed my smartphone in a lockbox, and was escorted to the ambassador's office.

Photos of Ambassador Kounalakis with political figures hung on the wall, and her assistant, Sheila, shared tales of typical embassy work as I waited to meet my lunch date. I sat in a blue-and-white-striped chair gazing at photos of Barbara Boxer, Nancy Pelosi, Madeleine Albright, Michelle Obama, and other trailblazing women in the world of politics. Soon I was escorted into the ambassador's oval office, which was complete with a china tea set and a view overlooking a manicured courtyard park with a children's playground. The meeting could not have gone better. The ambassador was gracious, intelligent, and thoughtful as she whisked me off to a lunch of pomegranate risotto with duck confit and herbal iced tea. Over our meal, we realized we had attended several of the same political events in the Bay Area and that we were potentially connected via more people than just our mutual Facebook friend.

What I enjoyed most about the visit was Ambassador Kounalakis's openness and willingness to meet with a stranger based on the recommendation of one friend. She gave me the gift of her time, and her insight and experiences in Budapest shaped the rest of my short trip. At lunch, she gave me sightseeing recommendations and explained what steps she had taken on the extraordinary path from her hometown of Sacramento, California, to the venerable capital of Hungary. It so happens that a lot of her success was rooted in her commitment to helping others, whether within her community in California or in the broader arena of global politics.

That experience demonstrates how social media have accelerated our natural abilities to make connections. In the old model of networking, connections were made in formal ways and typically one at a time. Communication methods such as phone calls and letters have lag times that make instant networking next to impossible. In the new model, social tools such as Facebook, Twitter, and LinkedIn allow us to connect less formally with many individuals instantaneously. It's also possible to understand the dynamics among communities of like-minded people based on interest, posts, and group affiliations. For example, it's always easier to connect via a warm introduction than a cold call. I'm quite confident that lunch with an ambassador would not have happened without the introduction from our mutual Facebook friend. Having a defined online brand or profile also makes connecting more likely, as credibility checks are just a click away.

One company that leverages the idea that having friends in common can improve your feelings of trust or potential connections is Airbnb. The website offers a service where guests and hosts can connect over an online platform to rent rooms, homes, and more around the world. I spoke with Joe Zadeh, who heads up product and innovation, and he said, "At first we integrated with Facebook because it was a way to reduce the barrier to trial, people could upload their social profiles quickly to use our site, and they didn't have to waste time filling in forms. But now the true value is that you can see how you're connected to people with listings around the globe." For example, Mr. Zadeh said, "if you want to go to Shanghai and both you and the potential host have uploaded your social connections, you can uncover who you know in common. Or you could join an alumni group and look up all the listings of people who attended the same university you attended and plan your trip based on connections."

Facebook and LinkedIn groups are also being used to break down geographic barriers. I belong to several groups: one for writers and another for social media enthusiasts, which have been incredible sources of focused, topic-based information. You may want to consider starting your own online community or group focused on your passions or values. The tune-up tip below provides insights to help get you started.

Tune-up Tip: Join an online community or attend a Meetup event.

One way to network regarding a topic is to host or attend a chat, forum, or dinner on the subject.

- Join a Facebook or LinkedIn group or start a group of your own.
- Search Meetup, an online network of local events. In my zip code, there are meet-ups on everything from website coding to single parenting.
- Attend a Grubwithus dinner and select a group based on your interests.

Job Prospecting Redefined

Technology has also redefined how we prospect for jobs, meet business contacts, and interview. The first interview I had when I was up for the position at Virgin America, in 2007, was conducted via a videoconferencing facility. That interview turned into another and another, and ultimately I was offered the position at the start-up airline. Today, a similar interview would be conducted over Skype or iPhone FaceTime or via Google Huddle.

Looking back, I recall another time in my life that also illustrates the difference between the old and new model of networking. After four years of college in Boston, I moved back to my home state of Minnesota and found a small apartment. A recession was in full swing, and jobs were hard to find. I spent my days and nights looking for a job. Thankfully, the receptionist at felony probation, where my mom worked, was on maternity leave, so I temped for the Hennepin County court system. At the job, I fended off a wide assortment of potential dates (a male stripper thought we were soul mates) and I borrowed the Wite-Out and photocopy machine to make copies of my résumé.

It was around that time that the power of networking started to impact my life and career path, though I wasn't quite conscious of it yet. On my days off and weekends, I'd make calls to potential employers and would send off letter after letter. My mailbox looked as though it was jammed with naked holiday cards missing their festive, seasonal stamps. Cream-colored envelopes with perfectly folded letters headed off to their potential contacts and to any job listing that sounded appropriate for a recent graduate with a business degree. To keep track of the inquiries and calls, I made a huge spreadsheet out of graph paper from my dad's basement office. I had a file folder for each inquiry, and I made notes on every call I made. I followed up. I sent thank-you notes. I read trade magazines and watched if an advertising agency or a firm was getting new business. If they were, I'd send off another résumé and tailored letter as soon as I could.

If I got an interview, I'd always ask for two additional contacts I could call on for further informational interviews. In hindsight, that was my first official attempt at networking, and though there were lots of jobs I didn't get—including a host for a local television station, a salesperson for Schwan's Ice Cream, and an array of entry-level jobs at Carlson Marketing Group, 3M, General Mills, and every advertising agency in Minnesota—I learned how to network and research the old-fashioned way.

There were no online applications, no emails, no Google searches, and no social media. This was old-fashioned networking paired with library research, constant reading, and a lot of stamp licking. Though I am not talking antiquity here, how we meet and network has dramatically changed even since then. The days of getting a job through a series of one-on-one interviews where you wear your blue suit aren't as common. Now your recruitment involves analysis of your personal profiles on Google, Facebook, and LinkedIn, group lunches, video chats, and other approaches, as well as the formal interview.

Using Email to Make a Connection

I picked up one example of how to effectively use email to network from T. J. Sassani, the CEO and founder of zozi, an adventure experience website. "One of my most recent hires was a new public relations person named Tian. She found my profile on LinkedIn and sent me an email that was so passionate I realized she could sell the company better than I could. I hired her on the spot."

If you are prospecting like Tian or trying to get an interview, you need to look for ways to break through the clutter of the numerous conversations people are exposed to daily. What is memorable about your pitch, email, or tweet? Are you being clear and direct? Is the subject line header catchy enough to grab someone's attention? Think creatively, and keep your passions and purpose in mind when you use online tools to communicate.

A mistake that people often make is not being specific. For example, have you ever sent a long email to a new contact without details on a proposed follow-up, request, or action item? If you are looking for an interview, are you clear with your request? Make sure your writing is concise, memorable, and typo-free. For example, a boring marketing email header for Virgin America could be "Fares starting at $49." Over time we found that the most successful emails and the ones with the highest open rate leveraged the witty Virgin tone of voice plus a clear fare message. Consider several examples sent for holiday sales:

- Our resolution? Slimmer fares. San Francisco flights from $49.
- No tricks, just treats. Sweet fares from $34.
- Book by 11:30AM PDT: Treat yourself to tricked-out flights from $39.

Next time you're sending an online communication, think about the details. Review your subject line or your 140 characters. Would you open it, read it, or retweet it? Consider if the receiver has time to read the content. And remember to include a clear, simple ask or closing statement, such as a meeting request or what advice you are seeking. If you don't get an answer to your email, do not give up. You might need to be more creative.

Jessica Stout, a marketing manager, landed an initial interview with me after she designed a Virgin America boarding pass with a personalized message to me. The boarding pass encouraged me to read her résumé, which included the fact that Ms. Stout had been on a television show called *The Amazing Race* and climbed Mount Kilimanjaro. Jessica's unique background, determination, drive, and passion for the position set her above numerous other applicants. She was overqualified to be my assistant but took the job to get her foot in the door and was promoted soon after joining the company.

Exercise 3: Conduct job-prospecting exercises.

If you're in the process of job prospecting, here are several online steps to take.

- Look for online sites and email lists that post job listings in your area of interest (e.g., TheLadders, LinkedIn etc.).

- Update your LinkedIn profile (very important).
- Update your résumé and bio.
- Ask contacts in your network for recruiter and interview referrals.
- Send an email to trusted friends and explain that you're looking for new opportunities.
- Prepare an updated list of references and ask for endorsements on LinkedIn.
- Review your passions to determine if you have passion-based revenue streams you can generate (e.g., you love photography, offer photography services).
- Secure social media handles (e.g.@portergale) as needed.

In summary, it is clear that technology has changed how we network and make connections. If you use technology wisely, you can use it to increase your feelings of virtual intimacy, find new contacts, and nurture global connections, and you can transform your job prospecting and networking. My advice is that you should embrace rather than shun the new online tools and social sites. If used properly, you can make new connections, improve your happiness, and impact your future prosperity.

Chapter 6: Summary

Step 6: Accelerate your connections with technology.

Tune-up Tip: Your network adds to your worth, so organize your contact information.

Exercise 1. Explore social media sites and use online research to find communities and connections.

Exercise 2. List three people you would like to meet.

Tune-up Tip: Join an online community or attend a Meetup event.

Exercise 3. Conduct job-prospecting exercises.

Top Tips

1. Expect the unexpected, and have a "can-do" attitude.
2. Do your homework on connections you'd like to make.
3. Use social media to make connections before and during events.
4. Grab social media handles and pages as needed.
5. Remember, the separation between contacts is diminishing.
6. Use Skype, iPhone FaceTime, and other technologies to reduce virtual distance.
7. Think like a marketer when using email.
8. Look at bios on social media for information when engaging in online dialogue.
9. Use social media and attend group functions after meetings and events to stay in touch.

7

Build Out Your Core

Cultivate Positive Relationships, Support Your Purpose

As your network builds, the way you interact and treat your professional and personal colleagues, especially in your core circle, will have a dramatic impact on your ability to achieve your purpose and find happiness and success.

Unlocking the hidden power of connections is not about doing a "blame game"; it's about looking at yourself and being the best you can be so you can approach the world with confidence and achieve happiness and success. The saying "Keep your side of the street clean," a common twelve-step program phrase, can also be applied to networking; it means to admit your faults, be honest, take the high road, show up, value your relationships, practice clear communication, and understand you can control your own actions but not the actions of others. It also means that as you build a team, you should remember to focus on your carefully defined passions and purpose. Keep your thinking free of clutter and distractions that can block your path. And remember to break down barriers that reduce the strength of your relationships, especially among your core circle of personal and professional contacts.

Your core circle is unlike other relationships in your life; the individuals in the circle are enormously important, but so is the circle itself. There are times to add people and occasions that require you to venture into the outer reaches of your network. Your core circle may include a business partner, a spouse, a best friend, and other relationships in your life. Your circle affects how you spend your time and where you socialize, your networking success, and ultimately your happiness. Outside your core circle is your network ring of influence, or your secondary circles. These rings of influence have a secondary, yet highly important, impact on your networking. Your goals are to build authentic, honest, emotionally based connections and to identify if you need any additional support or resources to help you realize your passions and purpose. My core circle includes my daughter, my mother, my sister, and several close girlfriends. My secondary circles include numerous business contacts, friends, neighbors, a financial adviser, cousins, mentors and mentees, and more.

Step 7: Cultivate relationships that support your purpose.

In this section, you will complete three exercises. In Exercise 1, you will define your core circle. In Exercise 2, you will overlay your core circle with your passions and determine if you need secondary support. And in Exercise 3, you will make a list of five people whom you value and plan to reach out to.

Before you start the exercises, here are some stories that demonstrate the power of having core and secondary circles that support your passions and ultimate purpose.

The Inner Circle: Getting Advice, Strength, and Funding from Friends

Melody McCloskey always knew she would "do something," but for several years her fear of failure held her back. "I was working long hours at Current TV. I loved software and computers but didn't know how I would fit into the business world. All my friends were founders of companies. We talked about business, fund-raising, launching prototypes; those became the only conversations we had." Ms. McCloskey had the idea for StyleSeat, an online booking portal for stylists and wellness services, two years before she launched the business. "Over time, my need to do it got stronger than my fear of failing. I had to do it. I knew I'd deeply regret it if I didn't start my company." In stealth mode, she broke down the business into steps and found a coder on Craigslist, recruited a cofounder, hired a designer, and told all of them, "Don't tell anybody." She and her partner put all of their savings into the business and lived from hand to mouth for a year.

By that point, Ms. McCloskey had generated a very large network in the technology and start-up space, as she "had been going to two events a day, about four times a week, to expand my circle. I always asked for advice, and soon the people I met became my social network too, as we had so much in common." One of the events Ms. McCloskey attended was LeWeb in Paris. She was with Travis Kalanick and Garrett Camp, the cofounders of Uber, an application-based car service company. They went sightseeing and decided to indulge in a four-star dinner. But Melody had no money because she had put everything into her business. She told me, "Travis looked at me and said, 'You're going through it. We know what it's like, and we think you're awesome. We'll do anything for you and will support you, but when you have a fancy jet you need to promise to help other entrepreneurs. And we're paying for dinner.'" She added, "It was one of the best dinners of my life. We sat next to Elton John, drank champagne, and talked about business. The support I received from friends is something that I think about every day." Ms. McCloskey's core and secondary contacts provided strategic advice and mentoring and became her first-round investors.

Melody is now inspired to give back and often has coffee with young entrepreneurs. "I've also gone from fearful to fearless. Since I now know what I stand for, I can do anything. I have tons of energy, and I think big. I'm where I am because of awesome friends, and I made a decision to ask for help. If Zappos can do it, why can't I? You're the only one who holds yourself back."

A Well-Defined Core Community: All Greeks Welcome

When chatting with Ambassador Eleni Tsakopoulos Kounalakis about her upbringing, I could easily see that her family forms the center of her core circle. "First and foremost is the family, after that community, then the church, and then anyone who liked Greek food was welcomed in." Ms. Kounalakis spoke fondly of her father, Angelo, who immigrated to California from a small village in Greece. "My father was a teenager when he arrived and realized that in the American system if you worked, got involved in the issues and the local campaigns, you could join into any community just by showing up."

From a young age, Ms. Kounalakis recalled that people were always "coming and going" in their home and that her Greek-American community in Sacramento "supported itself by using each other's shops, services and by creating a support system." From an early age, her father taught her to give back and to get involved. "I've been stuffing envelopes for causes since I was fourteen. That's what my parents believed in. I remember sending document after document over the fax machine—a cover sheet plus a flyer. I wouldn't stop until the fax machine inevitably broke or needed paper or more ink." She also shared one of her father's philosophies: "Do good things for the community, state and nation. It always starts there. Always be prepared to reach out and give." Ambassador Kounalakis told me how she had worked side by side with her father for eighteen years. He was a farmworker and then became a real estate developer. The ambassador added, "*The Sacramento Bee* said he did more to change the face of Sacramento than anyone."

Ms. Kounalakis noted that her father-in-law, also Greek, shares similar values and viewpoints. When he moved to the United States, the Greek-American community helped him find a place to live and gave him towels and dishes. Soon he saved enough money to buy a truck and took as many jobs as possible to pay off the mortgage. "The whole family knew the break-even day and when they'd have enough money to bring another family member over from Greece and buy another truck." Ms. Kounalakis added, "Your network or your community is everything."

Not everyone enjoys the support of a core circle based on shared heritage and shared economic interests. Over minestrone, I chatted with a single dad of three boys who had moved to California from South Africa. "I guess at the center of my circles are my dogs; they'll never leave"—he smiled—"and of course my boys." The well-educated businessman also included two close friends within his core circle and concluded, "I'd love to have a monthly meeting with like-minded dads to discuss parenting. I could use more support, because most of my family is in South Africa." You can build out your core circle based on interests and family type. For example, if a person is looking for more professional support, he or she may supplement his or her core circle with a business coach or mentor. Or if a person is working to overcome a barrier of substance abuse or nonproductive behavior, he or she may share his or her experiences and challenges with a trusted sponsor.

When thinking about your core and secondary circles, keep your passions and purpose in mind. For example, Dr. Jeffrey Halbrecht, an orthopedic surgeon, is very passionate about his Jewish heritage. As a dad of two small children, Dr. Halbrecht wanted to make sure his children were raised in a supportive, thriving Jewish community. As a start, he volunteered for the membership committee at his synagogue and started hosting "chats" at his home for prospective parents to learn more about the local Jewish elementary school. He looked at his circles, decided where he wanted to grow his connections and relationships, and got involved. If you want to build our your core circle, consider your heritage, the people in your existing circle, and your passions and make a plan to get involved and connected.

Exercise 1: Define your core circle.

Write down the list of people in your core circle. You may find that it includes one person, three, ten, a congregation, or a neighborhood. It doesn't matter if your list is short or long. The goal of defining your core circle is to determine if you need to nurture or add secondary relationships or activities to support your passions and purpose. Questions to ask:

1. Whom do you seek out for spiritual, emotional, medical, physical, or financial advice?
2. Whom would you reach out to if you had a flat tire or were changing jobs or career paths?
3. If you have a bad day, whom do you lean on?
4. Whom do you vacation or spend free time with?

It's important to recognize that your upbringing and family structure have a dramatic impact on your approach to connecting and your definition of your core circle. For example, Ms. Kounalakis's core and secondary circles are very well defined in part because of her upbringing and her family's strong ties to the Greek-American community. Remember, when thinking about your family history, look for cultural traits and community strengths to help you on your path to discovery and growth.

The Power of Family and Shared Connections

Hermione Way, originally from the United Kingdom, was a year old when her parents divorced. "My brother, Ben, who is five years older than me, was shipped off to be with my father, and I stayed with my mum. My brother was a troublesome child; Mum couldn't handle the two of us, so they split us up. Then my mum had a boyfriend and my dad remarried, so my brother had stepbrothers and stepsisters. We were like two separate families," she told me.

Hermione and Ben saw each other a couple of times a year, but that changed when they reconnected as adults. "When I was eighteen, I was on a gap year traveling, and Ben and I decided to meet in Thailand. We hung out for two or three months and found out we are so similar. I'm like him in a wig. We look the same, like the same music, we're so similar it's unreal." The reunited siblings went on crazy adventures, learned how to dance with fire, and "got on like best friends."

The two now share a home in San Francisco, have several businesses together, and are being featured in a television show. "He's techie, likes building things, and really ups my game. I'm into marketing, public relations, and branding. We're amazing separately, but together we're going to blow things up." Ms. Way recalled that she recently missed a flight home and realized all she wanted to do was get home to see her brother. "It was so unusual to have that feeling. I almost cried. I have always been on my own, and it's really grounding to have someone there for me." She added, "My mother was loving, but we didn't have a perfect household. Because it was hard, it gave me the hustle I needed to make something of my life."

Ben added his recollection of the period: "I was a very hyperactive child. I was the only child at playgroup that had to be supervised at all times. I was too much for Mum; one day she dropped me off at my dad's. First it was for the weekend, then the summer, and then I realized I wasn't going home to Mum and Mione." His story mirrored his sister's. "We were completely separate, she was my sister and I loved her, but we never had that bond." When Ben and Hermione reunited in Thailand, he found that "we were on the same level, we realized our brains worked the same way. If you had opened our cupboards, we would have had the same things; we're like a couple of squirrels, we both eat tons of nuts, Marmite, tea, and alcohol."

The brother and sister now share a home they call "The Villa" in San Francisco. "It's nice to have someone around that understands you, doesn't judge you, and can tell you you're not crazy. Mione talks to me and understands me in a way that no else ever has. Now I have family. It's a real balance; it's really nice. She is the most important person in my life."

Core and Secondary Circles and Job Transitions

The people in your core circle also greatly impact your professional relationships. When Rosemarie Ryan decided to leave her post as copresident at J. Walter Thompson, a global advertising firm, she admitted to being "terrified." Her emotional state was so unbalanced that her business partner, Ty Montague, told her, "Let me know when the real Rosemarie is back." For Rosemarie, the transition from global advertising president to running her own firm, called Co:, was possible because of her strong core and secondary circles. "I was overwhelmed with the outpouring of emotional support I received," she said. A card from Shelly Lazarus, the chairman of Ogilvy & Mather, made a lasting impression. "You are the boldest, bravest woman I've ever met," she wrote. "Whatever I can do, let me know." The card is symbolic of the support Ms. Ryan received from her friends and her peers.

In addition to emotional props, Ms. Ryan and Mr. Montague quickly started adding clients to their roster, all of which came by way of personal and business contacts, without the customary outreach through media or advertising. When I asked Rosemarie why her network is so strong, she said, "I always help when I can, I'm honest and I do what I say I'm going to do, and I care about the outcome.

"Staying at JWT would have been the cowardly thing to do," she added. "I followed my passion. It's important to get used to not being comfortable." Rosemarie's happiness and success were improved because of her strong network and her desire to create a collaborative environment.

Build Long-Term, Authentic Relationships

Another key to building core and secondary circle relationships is to understand the value of long-term relationships. Emily Olson, whom I met at a conference in Napa, moved to San Francisco from North Carolina in 2009 with her fiancé, Rob, to build their company. The duo curated Foodzie, an online portal and subscription service for gourmet foods that was sold to Joyus. "When we moved to San Francisco our business took off; people here are so collaborative and supportive. We've also learned the value of building long-term relationships," she said. For example, in her industry, she described June Taylor "as the godmother of jams and preserves." Ms. Olson met Ms. Taylor at her shop in a food market called the Ferry Building, purchased some of her jams, and pitched a collaboration idea. "Ms. Taylor was supportive but told me she doesn't work with any other sites." However, Emily kept buying jams, and several years later they were both asked to be judges on a preserve-tasting panel. They built a relationship and became friendly, and eventually Ms. Taylor's products were featured on the couple's website.

Ms. Olson cited a similar process developed with the entrepreneur and technology investor Kevin Rose. "We hosted a tasting at our office to teach people how to use spices and to share some of the medicinal benefits of tea. Kevin attended because he likes tea," she told me. "It turns out he lives two blocks and we live three blocks from an amazing tea lounge called Samovar Tea Lounge. We kept running into each other, a friendship developed, and he invested in our company."

I myself recently benefited, personally and professionally, from a long-term business relationship. On a trip to New York City late last year, I had lunch with a past colleague and friend. I worked with Christina Grdovic nearly twenty years ago at an advertising agency in SoHo, and she is now the publisher of *Food & Wine*. I told her about my book and several recent speaking engagements. After lunch, without my knowledge, Christina sent an email to Peter Bates, who organizes the annual American Express Publishing Luxury Summit, and recommended me as a speaker.

Several days later, I received an email from Mr. Bates requesting additional information. I called, and ironically Mr. Bates was in a cab with Christina, visiting clients in Mumbai, India. Christina later confessed, "It was strange, being in a cab halfway around the globe, and having you call a colleague who is sitting next to me." Mr. Bates and I discussed the event, and he booked me for it.

Five months later, I flew to West Palm Beach for the event and not only saw Ms. Grdovic but ran into several other contacts. At one dinner, I was seated at the head table between Chris Matthews, the host of MSNBC's *Hardball with Chris Matthews*, and Kenneth Chenault, the chairman and CEO of American Express. I chatted with my seatmates about politics, technology, online payments, social media, and family and even had a brief, humorous dialogue with Mr. Matthews about mimes. The lesson here is that when you skillfully nurture your network, you can increase the possibility of seeing returns multiply over time.

The Strength of Your Network: Advisory Panels

Anna Griffin, the founder and editor in chief of *Coco Eco Magazine*, similarly learned about the value of her core circle. "Several years ago I left a toxic marriage and a career in real estate that I could not connect to. Some people in the industry would trample their grandmother to get a listing." Anna took a new course and followed her passion and launched a magazine that combines sustainable fashion and beauty. Anna's magazine grew, and to support her efforts, she brought in a CFO who was part of a venture capital team. At one point, her partners were discussing a financial raise that would impact the ownership structure and her own stake in the company.

"Thankfully, I have four very close advisers, and I was able to go to them for advice." She'd picked them because they had "graduated from the school of hard knocks" and had achieved a certain level of success. "With their insight, I realized I didn't want to make the change, and ultimately I restructured my team," she said. "Within your own network is often the smartest place to look for talent. Contacts will show up when you least expect it." Anna continued, "It was a wake-up call. I was so focused on the magazine that I had my head in the clouds. It wasn't the luck of the stars; key supporters and allies emerged, and I made the right decision."

Strengthen Your Relationships: Learn to Communicate

Learning how to communicate is just as important as the contacts in your circles. When Vivian Walker Ball started an intense long-distance relationship, her mom wisely cautioned, "You can't be kissy all the time; you'll need to learn to communicate and express yourself in nonphysical ways." The relationship flourished, and Vivian and her husband, Mike Greentree, have now been married for more than ten years and have two young boys. Over the span of their marriage, Mike, who is a lieutenant commander and aviator in the navy, has been deployed overseas four times, twice for six months and twice for a year. Now a fifth deployment to Bahrain, in the Persian Gulf, is pending. To bridge the distance and preserve some degree of intimacy, the couple has learned to use Facebook, Skype, and letter writing to maintain a sense of connection.

The couple had to learn to express their feelings and decide what to share and what not to share. "I'm lucky," says Vivian. "Mike is old-fashioned, so he writes me a lot of love letters on stationery. For every three he sends me, he'll also write a handwritten letter to the boys. I've learned how to thrive and survive during deployment, and social media platforms really help." Vivian uses social tools not only to stay connected to Mike and other families but to find resources and crowd-source questions to other military families. The Department of Defense and the Department of Veterans Affairs have jumped into the digital age and train families how to use those tools with operations and security in mind. For Vivian and other military families, technology has transformed family communications—and sometimes with a novel personal touch. "We put a laminated picture of Mike on a stick, and we bring it everywhere. We took photos of Mike-on-a-stick at a pool, at barbecues, on a trip to the White House." Vivian instantly sends the photos to Mike from her iPhone. "He loves the pictures. It also has made his time away a game for the boys, and they feel more connected."

Vivian uses Facebook and has learned to manage her privacy and security settings to share with family or larger groups. "Many parents and grandparents enter the platform to see regular updates and postings about their children. If you see a photo, it gives you a sense that they're okay and secure." She talks emotionally about one R&R (rest and recuperation) homecoming. "We had just picked up Mike, and he was putting our three-year-old into the car. I turned and snapped a picture and put the image on Facebook. By the time we got home, we had over a hundred messages thanking Mike for his service. It was humbling, and you realize that you're not alone. Seeing photos of homecomings also reassures other military families that they'll eventually have their turn to dance."

To share what she has learned, Vivian now works with a nonprofit called Blue Star Families, which is dedicated to empowering and supporting military families and to helping them connect using today's tools and technologies. Vivian has found that actively networking with other military families, both online and offline, has strengthened her core and secondary circles while developing a large community with a shared sense of purpose. Here are other communication tips to consider applying to your core and secondary circles:

1. Avoid triangular conversations and nondirect dialogue (e.g., "Tell your mom to X").

2. Refrain from sending emails, texts, or tweets or leaving voice mail messages when angry or upset.
3. Remember that tone can be misinterpreted on many modes of communication.
4. Avoid using the BCC function in email, and keep dialogue honest, simple, and transparent.
5. Clarify often by saying "I hear what you're saying" or "Is what you're saying . . ." so it's obvious you are practicing active listening.

Exercise 2: Overlay your core circle with your passions to determine if you need secondary support.

The goal of this exercise is to determine if your core circle helps to support your passions or purpose. For example, remember Jen in chapter 1? She has a passion for fitness but realizes she needs support in achieving her goals. Her solution is to engage daily with a Nike+ app and to follow @nikerunning on Twitter, to help her stay motivated and on track. The benefit of this exercise is to identify where you can add support so you can live your passions and purpose. Below, I've identified relationships in my core circle that are supportive of my passions as well as secondary ways and activities I can pursue to nurture my passions.

Passion Support Chart			
Purpose	To inspire others to live productive lives by breaking down barriers and connecting with others.		
Passions	Storytelling	Health	Technology
Core Circle Support	Sister, Daughter	Friends, Daughter	Clients, Friends
Need Secondary Support? (Yes/No)	Yes (Classes)	Yes (Trainer)	Yes (Online Community)

1. Recall your barriers, defined passions, and purpose.
2. Look at the relationships in your core circle. Do any of the relationships in your core circle support or share your passions?
3. Identify and find secondary relationships, communities, programs, or apps to support your passions and purpose and to break down any barriers. Consider taking advantage of:
    • Online communities and apps
    • Twitter feeds to support your topic or passion
    • Membership organizations
    • Twelve-step programs
    • Coaches, mentors, and advisers
    • Spiritual or religious practices
    • Classes, workshops, and academic programs
    • New routines with current circle members or new friends

When thinking about your core and secondary circles, remember that they make up your lifelines, your go-tos, and the infrastructure or community that can help you support your actions.

The Value of Your Network: A Community Comes Together

When something bad happens to people in our core circle, harnessing positive productivity, a Give Give Get attitude, and the support of strong relationships in your core and secondary circles becomes more important than ever. It's also important to remember that often "luck is a residue of design," as noted by the baseball legend Branch Rickey. For example, if you have built a strong core circle, a community is likely to pull together if you are facing a time of need. Consider the story of my friend the actor Jeff Riebe.

The weekend of a milestone birthday, I was at the San Francisco airport waiting for Jeff to arrive on a flight from New York City. Jeff and I met in eighth grade at a church overnight, and we've talked almost daily since then. Over the years we have been roommates and confidants, sharing the highs and the lows of our dreams and disappointments. We held each other when our fathers died, and we rejoiced when either of us fell in love. We share passions for Scrabble, Ben & Jerry's Chunky Monkey, skiing, and the exuberance of lower Manhattan. When Jeff wasn't on the morning flight as scheduled, I knew instantly that something was wrong. I left a frenzy of messages. "Jeff where are you? I'm at the airport. I'm getting worried." Jeff is the type who organizes his sock drawer by color palette, and his penmanship looks like a perfect handwritten font. Jeff does not miss flights, and he always returns phone calls. I called an ex-boyfriend who lived in New York City and asked if he'd help me find him. A couple of hours passed, and he called back. "There was an accident last night in Midtown at Fifth Avenue near Jeff's apartment. The person involved is listed in critical condition, but I couldn't get the name." Soon the bad news was confirmed: Jeff was in critical condition at Bellevue Hospital. A drunk driver, speeding down Fifth Avenue, had run a red light and swerved to avoid hitting a taxicab. The car had jumped a curb and crashed into Jeff as he walked along the sidewalk after exiting a deli.

The impact left Jeff with extensive brain injuries, about fifty broken bones, shattered teeth, and lacerations from head to toe. Devastated and filled with fear, I packed a black dress and flew to New York City. Soon the hospital waiting room was filled with Jeff's family and numerous friends. Jeff was in a coma, and the doctors told us it was going to be touch and go.

The outpouring of love and support that surrounded Jeff filled the space with positive energy and hope in the days that followed. Jeff's mother, Margi, recalled, "I had no idea how many friends Jeff had. There were new visitors every day, all day. Jeff was never alone. His friends did so much." She temporarily moved to New York City, and his two brothers flew back and forth from Minnesota. Jeff's church conducted prayer circles, and friends and music surrounded him. Fund-raisers were held around the country, and thousands of dollars were raised to help mitigate his medical expenses. Meanwhile, the news from the doctors was bleak. Margi was told to think about organ donation and also to prepare for the possibility of Jeff being brain-dead and never emerging from the coma. "We had a lot to deal with, but I knew he'd wake up and knew he'd be okay," she said. His friends started making jokes about what his first words would be; most people thought he'd wake up with his cynical voice and say "What the f*%k." Fifty-six days after the accident, I received a call that Jeff had opened his eyes. He was waking from his coma. With a laugh, his mom shared that his first words had actually been "I'm peeing."

Jeff faced extensive physical therapy, but he adapted to living with a traumatic brain injury. "I had to relearn everything, from how to lift a finger to how to walk," he said. "I knew in my head I could do it. The most important thing was learning how to communicate." I'd fly out to feed him and hold his hand. After eleven months, Jeff was transferred to Minnesota to be closer to his family and so he could receive better rehabilitative care. At first he lived at the Courage Center, then he moved to a group home, and now, five years later, he again has his own apartment.

Most inspiring is that even with his challenges, Jeff has stayed true to his passions. He does yoga, volunteers at the acclaimed Guthrie Theater, wrote a script called *Honest*, and wants to start an artist's group to mentor gay youths. The challenges he has faced are monumental, but each day he lives as fully as possible.

"I am blessed to be loved by so many people," he told me several years after the accident. "I could not accomplish anything without my friends. The things that bring me the most happiness are family and true friendship." Reflecting on the accident, he observed, "I think I was getting smokes at the deli, so it's very true that cigarettes can kill."

Because I've known Jeff for years, I know that his core and secondary circles are strong. He exemplifies a Give Give Get attitude and has a wicked sense of humor. He always showed up, was the first to do dishes at parties, and once I found him sweeping my garage during one of his visits to California. He cares about his friends, and they cared about him when he most needed their support.

Jeff's story illustrates the magical and transformative power a community or network can provide at a time of need. The entrepreneur Jack Hidary once said, "A great society does not come from wealth. We've seen empires with great wealth that have fallen. A great society comes from the strong bonds. When community ties are strong, rates of crime are lower. When people are connected, they are happier and are more likely to give back."

Let People Know You Value Them: Taking Flight

A key to nurturing successful core and secondary circles is to verbally remind those around you or working with you that you value them. At some times in our lives, our core circle will be very influenced by the pursuit of our professional goals. Fred Reid, the founding CEO of Virgin America, had to put his core circle to a test as never before when the start-up airline faced a four-year battle with the Department of Transportation (DOT) to get to launch. "It's hard to explain how hard the original team worked. It was a four-year, 24/7 adrenaline rush. All the executives took pay cuts and big-time career risks to start the airline," Reid recalled. "At one point, we were eighteen hours away from not making payroll. Some members of the board wanted us to lay people off. I said, 'We cannot do that. We have believers here, let's not make disbelievers of them.'" That wasn't the first nor the last time he would put the needs of the company's core circle first.

I remember a video, *Making of Virgin America*, which we shot when I joined the company. The filmmaker said to Reid, "You've got some kind of cult here. Every person I interviewed cried because they care so much." Reid said, "At the core, I cared. You want to give, as you want to get and treat others, as you want to be treated. You don't have to ask about their families or their dogs, but people can honestly tell when you care. Those people all took a risk to be at the airline.

"After almost four years, the company received yet another tentative disapproval from the DOT. It listed fifty-four conditions, and my resignation was number fifty-two." Reid recognized that the competitive set was pulling every string to "keep us from flying." The newest roadblock was that Sir Richard Branson, who is not a U.S. citizen, had hired Reid, and there were claims that Reid might be beholden to foreign interests. Reid laughed at the accusations, but after consulting with the legal department he told his board of directors, "You may not get an airline with me. But if you get me without an airline you'll lose $480 million and 788 people will lose their jobs." It was reluctantly decided that Reid would step down, and ultimately the airline received approval for its first flight on August 8, 2007.

"I felt like I had been evicted from the clubhouse. But then I said, it's not a personal tragedy and it's not a professional tragedy." He realized that if he did things right, there was a good chance the airline would succeed. He'd joined Virgin to start an airline, and he had. Although Reid doesn't think of himself as a religious or spiritual individual, he did say that living in India helped him gain perspective. "I admire the way Buddhists think about acceptance, and sometimes it's good not to get too attached to things. In my life I've learned that things always seem to make sense. Gratitude is a huge part of my mind-set."

Reid did what it took to make sure that his professional core circle remained strong. From the small actions of caring about his team to the monumental decision to resign as CEO, he took the steps needed to support his professional core circle. In the end his conscience-driven decision opened new doors, and he became the president of Flexjet, a private jet travel company based in Texas.

During my time at Virgin America, I used many phrases and mantras to build the passion and connectivity of our core team. The commonalities among the phrases are optimism, connection, and praise. Don't forget how important it is to let the people in your circles know they are valued. Asking for opinions on topics, making eye contact, and many other little actions can make a big difference. Porter-isms I used, provided by the Virgin America marketing team after I departed, include:

- Raise the bar.
- Fight mediocrity.
- You're a rock star.
- Double high five.
- Make it happen.
- See the good.

These phrases may sound familiar, but the impact of valuing your core and secondary teams will be large. Find a way to express your appreciation that fits your desired tone from your Funnel Test.

Exercise 3: Make a list of three to five people whom you value and reach out to them.

This may seem obvious, but often we forget to tell people in our core or secondary circles that we value or appreciate them. Make a list of three to five people and express your gratitude to them through a call, coffee date, or handwritten note.

Circle-Damaging Behaviors:
Trash Talk, Egotism, Hierarchical Thinking

It's also important to know that negative behaviors or comments can quickly disrupt and kill connections and erode your network. Among them are an aggressive tone of voice, degrading your connections in front of peers or friends, using hierarchical titles unnecessarily, or making dictatorial statements such as "This is a monologue, not a dialogue" or "This is not a democracy." This is an example of the old, autocratic style of management and not reflective of the new collaborative model that supports cocreation and innovation. Often there are key decision makers, but team-work and collaboration are crucial ingredients of networking and core-circle success.

If you find yourself yelling at or putting down your peers or family members, my suggestion is to look back at chapters 1 and 2 and try to determine if there are behaviors that are holding you back. What behaviors or habits do you need to examine and change to transform your style and move you into a more ef-fective form of relationship building? Another behavior trait to watch for is gossiping or putting others down. Again, if you see these in yourself, take a look back at part I and do the inner work to move into a healthier, more productive style of networking. For example, after we had worked together on a film for several years, my coproducer initiated a miniroast that humiliated me in front of a packed theater at our opening-night screening. It may be that her intention was to bring humor to the screening, but I sank in humiliation as she detailed "all the scenes of Porter that you didn't see in the film."

I admit that I haven't always practiced what I preach. It's easy to get sucked into office gossip or to put others down in attempt to elevate your own self-worth. But remember, to unlock the hidden power of connections, networking is looking at *you* first so you can have better *we* relationships.

In summary, it's important to define your core and secondary circles so you can determine if you need to supplement your existing relationships to nurture your passions and purpose and break down your barriers. Develop communication styles that work for you, and create positive environments. Don't forget to first look at your own behaviors if your relationships start breaking down. You can't control the actions of others in your circles, but you can control your own actions, and you can choose to react in productive ways by keeping your side of the street clean.

Chapter 7: Summary

Step 7: Cultivate relationships that support your purpose.

Exercise 1. Define your core circle.

Exercise 2. Overlay your core circle with your passions to determine if you need secondary support.

Exercise 3. Make a list of three to five people whom you value and reach out to them.

Top Tips

1. Avoid triangular conversations.
2. Clarify often by saying, "I hear what you're saying" or "Is this what you're saying . . ."
3. Consider adding support from online communities, apps, twelve-step programs, and more.
4. Let people in your core circle know you value them.
5. Use positive mantras to motivate and reinforce positive behavior.
6. Avoid trash talk, egotism, and hierarchical thinking.

8

Power Pockets

Define the Places, Events, and Groups
That Accelerate Networking

Look at environments, clubs, and events to see how they can accelerate or diminish your efforts and ability to live your passions and purpose.

If you think of your network as a web of interconnected relationships, it is important to look at where you could get stuck and where you can accelerate your efforts. For example, if you are in an environment that sucks the life out of you or leaves you feeling depressed, you probably need to do an audit of what you can and can't change in the situation. Or if your personality conflicts with your role, you may need to make adjustments to bring about higher performance or to learn how to cope. For example, if you make decisions based on intuition but you're in an environment that values data and analytics, you may need to make adjustments. In this chapter we will look at the *where* and *with whom* of your efforts. We'll review the importance of your work space and the benefits of what I call "power pockets": places and events that accelerate networking and support your passions or purpose.

Step 8: Visit power pockets to accelerate networking.

This chapter includes two exercises. In Exercise 1, you will define two power pockets to visit. In Exercise 2, you'll learn how to evaluate the potential return on connecting within a potential power pocket event or group.

Are You in the Right Environment?

As you start this chapter, consider where you are, what you do, and whether you're in the right environment. Your physical space and the people around you will impact your output and productivity. For example, when Ann Winblad of Hummer Winblad Venture Partners finished college, she was offered several jobs in her home state of Minnesota. She graduated and ended up taking one at the Federal Reserve Bank, working there for thirteen months. Unfortunately, the environment didn't support her innovative approach to business. "I thought everyone would be hard-charging and would get there early and stay late. I was looking for a competitive environment where we would try innovative things." Ms. Winblad described the setup like a company out of central casting. Her cubicle was in the "sexiest" building in Minneapolis, off Nicollet Mall, the famed street where Mary Tyler Moore threw up her cap in the opening sequence of her eponymous sitcom.

One day Ms. Winblad asked a coworker where he went from 12:00 to 2:30 every day, and he said, " I ride my bike home, have lunch, and then I watch *I Dream of Jeannie*, drink a beer, and ride back to the office." After she questioned him about his extended break, he added, "No one notices, and there is a strain on compute time [because of heavy demand] during that time of the day." Ms. Winblad decided to conduct her own stealth flexible work time experiment with her section mates to streamline compute time and software usage during peak periods, thus flattening demand peaks and increasing productivity. At the end of the test period, the results were "stunning." The results of the test were presented up the chain of command, all the way to the bank president, and ultimately her boss took credit for the effort and received a promotion. After that incident and a disagreement about graduate school course costs that the bank was reluctant to reimburse for a rather baroque reason, Ms. Winblad realized that the company's robotic approach to process and progress would only hold her back from thinking creatively. She convinced three other employees to join her, and they started their own software business called Open Systems, which was successfully acquired for "a significant amount of money" several years later.

According to her, the success of the foursome was due to hard work, extraordinary insight into programming, a passion to excel, and the chemistry of the team. "It was a bit revolutionary and maybe overkill, but we hired a psychologist to interview us and new potential employees to make sure our hires were a good fit with the company. The biggest problem we had was that no one ever left and some turnover is good for a company." The psychologist also interviewed the founders during the acquisition phase to understand who was ready to scale and who wanted to sell. Ms. Winblad told me that she'd kept her psychological profile for a long time and had read it once in a while "to remember this is me."

Matthew Hinde, an executive recruiter, also thinks about environment when matching candidates to opportunities. "There are a range of cultures from places like Dropbox, where people wear sandals and music is playing, to Google, which is relaxed but polished, to places like BlackRock and iShares, which are very proper and people wear ties. The trick is not to prep people too much; you want them to be themselves. I joke it's like Match

.com; sometimes I'm wrong and it's a good fit, but typically in my gut I can tell if a candidate is right for an environment." He added that the past also helps to predict the future. To gain insight, he asks interviewees what cultures they have excelled in in the past. When looking at a new opportunity or environment, you may want to ask these questions:

1. Is it collaborative or competitive?
2. Does it make you feel drained or inspired?
3. Is anyone laughing or having fun?
4. Does it feel innovative or staid?
5. Can I add value to the situation?

If part of your networking goal is to find new employment, chances are you've already dusted off your résumé, are scanning Craigslist, researching companies, talking to recruiters, and hopefully interviewing. Interviewing and talking to recruiters is a wise step to take that can help you uncover your strengths and tell you if you're ready for the job market.

When I was considering leaving Virgin America, I fielded a call from the leadership recruiter of a large Silicon Valley technology firm. The recruiter's praise was solid, and the reputation of the company was off the charts. "What the heck," I said, "I'd love to chat with your team." During my seven-interview, three-day process, I learned a lot about my personality type and myself. The interviews forced me to think about the *where* and *with whom* that inspire me to be most productive. After several interviews with engineers, my last interviewer asked, "What is your Myers-Briggs type?" "I'm social, driven by emotions and intuition. I love data, digital media, and technology but also believe in gut decision making. Does that help?" I asked, smiling. The interviewer didn't look pleased. Not surprisingly, the recruiter called and told me that I wasn't perceived as quantitative enough for the job. I'd known the job wasn't a good fit, but I also knew that it is important to use opportunities like that one for growth and learning. Here are several questions to ask prior to taking on a job or new work project.

1. Does the project support my purpose and passions?
2. What types of environments and cocreators give me inspiration?
3. Are there facets of my personality that I should seek to improve, change, or grow?
4. Will I learn or improve my skills in this role?

Be authentic, but always attempt to read a situation; network and communicate with a style that fits the needs of the interviewer or contact. For example, if a new contact does not offer any personal information, he or she may relate better to facts, figures, and data. In such a situation, you'll most likely be more successful speaking about your specific accomplishments rather than telling a personal story or sharing emotional ideas or concepts. Interviews are not just a way for a company to get to know you but a way for you to get to know yourself and to help you sort out your likes and dislikes and learn how you relate to new people.

Ms. Winblad also had some thoughts on connecting: "You have to use caution, but I think it's important to try to reach out to connect on a personal level. We really don't need nerd number 508,002 in a room. We're not playing *Jeopardy!* or trying to prove that we know all of the state capitals or the population of the world." She added, "We need to stop proving how smart we are and have a little fun. You spend so much time at work; it is where you can build your friendships. So why not connect and make a new friend?" She mentioned, "When everyone's trying to prove how smart they are, I will often ask a personal question. For example, if I see you have a screen saver of a dog, I may share that I have a dog too. Connecting makes meetings more enjoyable."

In addition to your environment, it's important to have a work space that meets your needs. If you're in between jobs or starting a business, Wi-Fi-enabled public spaces and collaborative work spaces are a great option to investigate. Why is your work space important? It sets a tone, can provide inspiration, and in some cases can even impact your output. Tom Stone, a violinist with the Cypress Quartet, described environment as the "fifth instrument." Tom and his partners go to extensive lengths to find both practice and performance spaces that help bring their classical pieces to life. He said, "I need an instrument that can respond to my commands, and I need a room that reinforces and amplifies that so we can bring the emotions of the composers to life."

Rosemarie Ryan, a cofounder of Co:, also feels the physical work space is a key to culture, productivity, and connecting. "At my last job, the first thing I did was remove the doors from my large corner office," she said. "I'm not interested in a culture where people count ceiling tiles to show how senior they are. I like a physical space with no hierarchy, where people can be open-minded and work together. I don't want people hiding behind walls." So take a look at your work environment, and complete the tune-up tip below.

Tune-up Tip: Conduct a work space review.

Is your space adding to or detracting from your networking and collaborating? Do you have the tools needed to be efficient? Are you organized? Don't let a work space review overwhelm you, but do a quick audit to make sure your environment is helping you live your passions and purpose. Several items to audit:

1. Is your desk/chair ergonomically correct?
2. Do you have adequate light?
3. Do you have access to needed tools (high-speed Internet, printer, etc.)?
4. Do you back up your files and your contact information?
5. Are you using apps to make your life more efficient?

Regarding the last point, as the distribution of smartphones and personal electronic devices increases, app usage will continue to rise. For example, there is an app that can synchronize your Facebook and iPhone contacts. However, because apps change often, it is best to check reviews and recommendations to find versions that will work for your needs. There is a full list of apps and descriptions on the Apple iTunes Store and on the Chrome Web Store.

The Evolution of Power Pockets: From Country Clubs to Co-op Spaces

When you review your primary work environment, you should also consider if you spend time in what I call power pockets. In the old world, power pockets were synonymous with alumni or country clubs. Today, meet-ups, events, coworking spaces, and online communities are the new power pockets, or places where connections, conversations, and relationship-building efforts are in high gear. Some are free, and some have fees or membership structures. The key is to analyze the potential gains and judge them according to your purpose. Consider Jen from chapter 1: she spent $65 to attend a seminar where she gained confidence, met five contacts, and learned specific information in the area of her purpose. That's a solid return. I myself attended a writer's workshop where I ultimately met the agent who represents me. That's a fantastic return.

To contrast the power pockets of today and yesterday, during the development of this book, I was invited to the Harvard Club in New York City for several meetings. The prestigious venue, with a bar, restaurant, meeting rooms, and even a barbershop in the basement, is a members-only club. Wingback leather chairs, historical-looking portraits, and a coat check fill the lobby. A no-paper and no-laptop rule is enforced in the dining room on the main floor. Up a grand staircase, a meeting space with a bar and tables that would serve nicely for a poker tournament are filled with suit-wearing folks talking about investments, politics, and business deals. The space, which is still a power pocket and a delight to visit, is symbolic of old-world networking. Transactional meetings at country clubs, golf outings, and alumni clubs are still filled with deals discussions, job offers, and high-level connecting. But today, you can find options both offline and online that can provide the backdrop to accelerated networking and connecting.

Grind, off Park Avenue South in New York City, is representative of the new power pockets and the growing number of coworking spaces. The bright, modern, open-air loft looks like a modern-day library that married a coffee shop. The venue provides a networking opportunity, a way to keep start-up office costs minimal, and a stimulating alternative to a home office. Sleek white chairs, a cement floor peppered with orange-square rugs, several conference rooms, and an Intelligentsia coffee and tea station fill the space. A transparent box filled with outdated symbols of yesterday including a rotary phone, a fax machine, a Rolodex, cutoff ties, time sheets, and a Walkman doubles as a coffee table. This membership-only space is billed as a "friction-free, digital community and work space for awesomely talented and interesting people." A poster in the lobby states, "Grind is dedicated to taking all the frustrations of working the old way and pulverizing them to a dust so fine it actually oils the wheels of the machine."

Benjamin Dyett, one of the co-owners behind the space, said, "We're not in the real estate business: we're in the community-building business. The reason people show up is because they feel at home and know being here helps them to be better and more productive." The team behind the space curates the membership base to make sure the community is diversified and thus collaborative, not competitive. "If everyone in the space was an app developer, it wouldn't work," he told me. Grind also hosts a morning breakfast series with speakers such as Fred Wilson of Union Square Ventures and Sara Horowitz of Freelancers Union. "We look for ways to help people to do their best work. We also have a private section on our website where members can post a profile, a picture, and what expertise they have to offer and what collaboration or support they might need." Mr. Dyett noted that the efforts of members have extended beyond just work collaborations. "Several people that met here organized the first TEDx Harlem [an independently organized speakers' series], which was a huge success. They planned the entire thing here, so we sponsored the event too."

Coworking spaces such as Grind are popping up in markets across the country. In Reno, Nevada, Mike Henderson, a designer, joined a collaborative work space and collective called Reno Collective Coworking. "It's great because we can bounce ideas off each other," Mike told me over drinks. His collective adds a dose of productive learning by hosting "lightning rounds," four-minute PowerPoint competitions. Participants hone their presentation skills by making humorous speeches on topics ranging from mustache facts to skiing with babies. The collective also encourages musicians to play in its space for visibility and community building. Interestingly, the dividing line between professional and personal networking increasingly overlaps in this type of space.

Wi-Fi hot spots can also be power pockets for networking. For example, I recently spent the day plugging in at Ace Hotel on

Twenty-ninth and Broadway in Manhattan. At least fifty hipsters filled wingback chairs and lined a communal table that was peppered with power outlets and reading lights. A photo of Albert Einstein hung in the corner, and wallpaper made of graffiti lined a grand stairwell. Some folks were solo workers and sported Dr. Dre headsets; others engaged in laughter or business-filled conversations. A woman in patterned tights and black-rimmed glasses sat next to me with a heavy white ceramic coffee cup. A small sign on the table read, "Love your neighbor but keep an eye on your belongings." Beatles music played, and conversations could be heard in every corner. The Ace Hotel is more comfortable than Starbucks and not stuffy. It was a perfect power pocket and I was able to enjoy the lobby, while accessing email on my smartphone, without being a guest at the hotel.

Exercise 1: Identify two to three power pockets to visit.

Think about your community or places that you visit for travel, identify two to three power pockets, and make an effort to visit or work out of a location that's not your office. Consider Wi-Fi free zones, collaborative work spaces, reunions, meet-ups, tweet-ups, local chamber of commerce groups, speed networking events, and more.

Events, Conferences, and Meet-ups: Where Socializing and Growth Intersect

One person who understands the value and power of industry events is Ido Leffler, a cofounder of Yes To Carrots, a popular skin care brand. When Ido and his partner were starting their business, cash flow was tight. "In our industry, there is a massive industry conference in Bologna, Italy. I knew the biggest decision makers would be there, but we didn't have the money for a booth or to do an event. Usually, there's a VIP room for the bigwigs and large manufacturers. My goal was to get into that room," he told me.

He flew around the globe and made dozens of calls, and one contact lead to another. A friend of his named Claudio knew one of the organizers. "Somehow I scored a ticket and made it into the room. I wore a bright orange sweater that you could have seen from the moon, let alone the other side of the room. Mindy Grossman, the CEO of Home Shopping Network (HSN), walked right into me. It was crowded and there was no place to sit, but I presented to her. We made a deal right there, sitting on the floor, and three months later we were on the air. That day, I closed four deals that we still have six years later," he said.

Attending an event is how I met Tim Ferriss, the author of *The 4-Hour Workweek* and *The 4-Hour Body*. Tim and I were on a panel about social media with the entrepreneur Kevin Rose. After the session, Tim approached me and gave me a gift card for $100, explaining it was so I could make a donation to DonorsChoose .org, an online charity that helps fund projects in schools across the country. Wow, talk about living a Give Give Get attitude! As a result of Tim's generous act, the ripple effect included the development of a promotional campaign at Virgin America that raised $50,000 for DonorsChoose.org, from which 83 school projects were funded and 9,718 students were positively impacted. On a personal level, Tim then invited me to several events, where I made an array of new friends, and a contact in Tim's circle gave me the boost I needed to write this book.

Experiential Connecting at The Lobby

Events come in all shapes, sizes, and forms. One person who has developed a successful event formula is David Hornik, a venture capitalist with August Capital. Half a dozen years ago, Mr. Hornik decided to "make an event that fixed all the things that I thought were broken with conferences." He noticed that the bulk of great conversations at conferences were taking place in lobbies and bars during off-hours and that it was often hard for people to connect authentically. So he created The Lobby, an invitation-only conference for players in the technology and digital media fields. The Lobby conference had no speakers or panels, just experiences designed to promote deeper conversations and relationships.

One of Mr. Hornik's innovations was to rethink the conference attendee list. "In the past, you'd get a list of attendees by name or company. I could have spent hours looking for Porter Gale, assuming you were a man." He went on, "The first year of The Lobby, I asked everyone to make introductory videos before the conference, and I loaded them on iPods—one for each attendee." The videos ranged from webcam introductions to homemade music videos to comedy skits. He added, "I made a music video with a song written by my son. It featured my family members wearing logoed hats from groups that are important to us, from sports teams to shows to companies I've invested in to the sponsors of the event. It showed who I am but also communicated that family is important to me. Dick Costolo made a very funny video sitting in a dilapidated office full of boxes; he was riffing about selling Feedburner to Google and that despite the appearance he really had an excellent office and an excellent title. It was hysterical." Since that first conference, Mr. Hornik has used baseball trading cards, an interactive app, and even high-school-yearbook-themed materials to help conferencegoers connect. "The first year, we had dozens of people on the same plane heading to the event. Folks were leaning into the aisles, chatting about each other's videos. The connecting started before they even got to the event."

The Lobby has always taken place in a warm location; beach gatherings and games are the norm. "I wanted an environment based on collaboration. If you're wearing shorts and hula hooping, job titles and posing go out the window," said Mr. Hornik. Because the event is invitation only, he admitted that his biggest challenge has been figuring out how to say no. He invites people he wants to stay connected to or who have been referred by other attendees. He has learned that it is as important to have "no jerks" at The Lobby as it is to have big-name executives. "There is one person who refuses to play the games, and I may have to take him off the list. I want a level playing field where people can connect.

"The Lobby is about relationships, but business deals have been done, top people who met at The Lobby have moved from eBay to LinkedIn and Google to Facebook, and we've had amazing conversations," he said. No tweeting or social media posting is allowed, to encourage open dialogue, but he did share a few topics from a recent conference: "We talked about everything from the future of music copyright law to what can we learn from the failure of Myspace." His formula is working; this year's conference sold out within an hour of invitations being sent. "I've learned networking isn't a dirty word; it's really a great way to stay connected with my friends in the industry and to meet the people that my friends like. If they like them, I usually like them," he told me. "We're all going to be in this business for a couple of decades, so we might as well have fun and build great relationships."

Speed networking events are another interesting if exhausting way to meet contacts. For example, travel industry professionals can attend Virtuoso Travel Week, a four-day speed networking event, and have a hundred four-minute pitch appointments each day. In 2011, I attended a speed networking session at the American Express Publishing Luxury Summit at the Breakers Hotel in Palm Beach, Florida.

In a grand ballroom with oversized chandeliers, arched ceilings, and a large time clock, power networkers filled tables for three-minute pitch sessions. Each person had a box of business cards and optional visual materials. Like a grown-up version of musical chairs, if your back was to the clock you stayed stationary and if you faced the clock you moved when a timer went off. I was flanked by LeBaron Meyers, the vice president of strategic partnerships from UrbanDaddy, and a woman representing the Wakaya Club & Spa, a luxury private island resort in Fiji. In less than an hour, I collected fifteen business cards. Some of my miniconversations included: a dialogue about website design with a contact from Bal Harbour Shops; questions about social media from the vice president of marketing at ROHL Collection; questions about digital media and luxury buyers from the CEO of Buccellati, a high-end jewelry and watch company; and a request to speak at an event in San Francisco from a contact I had previously met in Paris.

There are ways to attend pay-for-play-type events or to review content without being a speaker or paying large entry fees. For example, TED, an invitation-only conference with a waiting list, allows independent producers to host similar events, called TEDx, around the globe. Janine Shiota, an event producer who typically pulls together more than twenty events a year, curates TedxPresidio on a pro bono basis. "I'm very interested in technology, social entrepreneurialism, and finding out about trends," she told me. "It's guaranteed that something amazing will happen when you bring together six hundred people for a day of dialogue. It is like throwing a pebble in the water and seeing what waves it will make." Video content from TED sessions is often streamed live or available online for public viewing. With this in mind, think about your passion, purpose, or industry and do your homework to find relevant events and online content opportunities. Event opportunities are wide-ranging and happening everywhere, every day.

In 2011, I made a presentation at TEDx La Jolla about the power of meeting people in spontaneous ways. Other speech topics ranged from childhood obesity to new reading techniques, and presenters included everyone from a teenager with cystic fibrosis to a group of children who had created a petition for peace. The musical acts ranged from Howie Day to a concert pianist and a violin prodigy. At the event, I met a woman who studies gorillas, a man who had been a child actor in Israel, and a couple who creates cause-oriented travel experiences. Consider all the new contacts you could meet and ideas that might be discussed at the next event you attend. Your network and your level of happiness and creativity will likely grow in relation to your connecting efforts. Or, like Janine, you might even consider hosting your own events. We'll talk more about this in chapter 9.

Exercise 2: Evaluate the connecting return on investment of potential events.

Prior to paying an entry fee or signing up for a high-cost event, ask yourself:

1. Will the event inspire me in the area of my passions or purpose?
2. Will I meet potential future professional or personal contacts?
3. Do I know anyone who has attended the event in the past?
4. Is event content available online for free?
5. What do I hope to achieve at the event?
6. Do I have the time and resources to attend without increasing my financial or mental stress?

In addition to attending events, it is also important to consider the impact geography can have on your success, productivity, and happiness.

The Impact of Geography: Location, Location, Location

Joe Marchese of Fuse Networks lives in New York City and partakes of the whirlwind schedule that defines life there. The day I met Joe, he told me, "Today I had six meetings, a lunch, took some clients to a Katy Perry concert, and attended a dinner with fifteen friends. You could never do this in Los Angeles or San Francisco because of geography. I'm so productive here and always get so much done." For Joe, the ease of zipping around Manhattan has increased his productivity and his ability to nurture his network. He's not stuck in a traffic jam or crossing a city to get to appointments.

Ryan Graves, of Uber, had a similar sentiment about San Francisco after he moved to the area from Chicago. For Mr. Graves, it wasn't the physical miles of his location but rather the energy of the city that impacted his productivity and mind-set. "Chicago was great, but I worked so I could live for the weekend. The goal was to go big on Friday night. It's not like that here because everyone wants to be productive over the weekend." When you're looking for a power pocket or place to live, consider your geography and its potential impact on your productivity. Remember Melody McCloskey in chapter 7? What would have happened if she had lived in Los Angeles rather than San Francisco while building her technology start-up?

You don't have to live in a major metropolitan area to find or create a thriving community, but you do need to consider whether you're in an area that can support your passions or purpose or have the ability to do so virtually. Jeff Slobotski, a community builder, entrepreneur, and connector, started a blog called Silicon Prairie News to profile entrepreneurs and innovators and help people in the Midwest thrive and make connections. "I'd hear about people doing amazing things, like a local design shop that was doing great work, and nobody knew about it. I wanted to share their stories to inspire people and foster more collaboration over time," he said. "For a while, I just had my blog, but the effort kept growing and there were more and more stories. We also started doing smaller events and saw the value of offline connecting, so we launched Big Omaha." Big Omaha, billed as "accelerating serendipity," is a networking conference and speakers' series that brings innovators together. Jeff said the focus of the conference is "organic conversations and connections."

Jeff, whom I met on Twitter, now employs a dozen people, and he has built a thriving business. He told me, "My wife knew I had to do this before I did. My real goal is to connect people and to help invigorate the Midwest. I know it's a five- to ten-year process, but I'm excited to see things happen. It's not about me, it's about our amazing community." Jeff's success is fueled by his passion and his authentic and honest approach. His philosophy is "Don't be a pest, be honest and be true." He tells potential speakers, "Please come inspire us and kick us in the butts."

Mastermind groups, clubs, and networking organizations can also provide great power pocket opportunities. Gordon Tucker, a start-up investor and former CEO of several companies, said that being involved in the Young Presidents' Organization (YPO), a networking organization of entrepreneurs, corporate executives, and family-business owners, has had a significant impact on his life. "It's like a personal board of directors; we have monthly confidential forum meetings with a group of twelve members and are encouraged to share equally about work, personal, and family issues." Mr. Tucker told me that he has turned to the group for everything from business advice to travel tips. "When I send an email to the group, answers roll back within minutes. It's very inspirational to have a peer group that you can rely on to support you and trust with confidential information." He added, "You become very close to people when you share your most intimate secrets. You never feel isolated when you belong to a group like this."

Connecting with Community: The Power of Groups

Even with potential differences and varying personalities in mind, it is important to realize that with effort even the most unlikely people can find ways to connect and benefit from interaction. In an interview, Dr. Allison Belger, a psychologist and the author of *The Power of Community: CrossFit and the Force of Human Connection*, told me, "When we find a common ground or situations that break down socioeconomic or demographic barriers, everything else dissipates."

Dr. Belger related stories from her experience taking a seventy-five-day course with the National Outdoor Leadership School in Patagonia: "It rained every day, we were wet, hungry, and I had to do a lot of soul-searching. At times I felt like I'd get hypothermia. It was powerful to learn to rely on people I would otherwise never have met. You're forced to see what you can offer each other and what you can learn from the connection." She added that the experience had helped her to be open when she met her husband, TJ. "We joke that growing up I was at a tea party when he was working in a lumberyard. I'm from an affluent background, and his parents were divorced with no money. I went to fancy schools, and he was a bartender and personal trainer who drove a motorcycle. But because of the kind of person he is, when you get down to it, none of those things matter. My life with TJ has taught me to be more open." Dr. Belger and TJ now own a number of CrossFit gyms in Marin County, California.

"Over and over, at the gym, we've seen incredible things happen," she remarked. "There is something that happens in groups that can catapult people in their lives in a way that was not happening before. People have lost weight and gained confidence, shed poor relationships, changed their eating habits, and even become more social. Many studies show that social connections and friendships do something for our bodies. There is even research demonstrating that people who are isolated fare more poorly with regard to disease, poverty, and illness than people who are socially integrated. If you get connected, you can live more healthfully and longer. It doesn't have to be about CrossFit; it can be any program or endeavor that fosters community or a shared experience with commitment, discipline, or sacrifice and makes us need each other and learn in a different way."

In summary, to accelerate your networking, always consider the *where* and the *with whom* of your efforts. Shake it up by visiting power pockets, consider the impact of your geography on your purpose, and look at personality types when interviewing or attending meetings. Remember that under the surface, there is learning to be had from every connection. Look for similarities, not differences, and you'll improve your chance of making positive connections.

Chapter 8: Summary

Step 8: Visit power pockets to accelerate networking.

Tune-up Tip: Conduct a work space review.

Exercise 1. Identify two to three power pockets to visit.

Exercise 2. Evaluate the connecting return on investment of potential events.

Top Tips

1. Avoid environments that bring you down.
2. Determine the value you can bring to a situation.
3. Explore coworking spaces and free Wi-Fi hot spots.
4. Attend events, conferences, and meet-ups to build your network.
5. Consider the impact of your location on your productivity.
6. Remember that we can all learn from one another.
7. Look for similarities rather than differences to strengthen connections.

9

Hub Players

Find and Learn from Connectors Who Belong on Your Team

Create value and opportunity by embracing highly networked individuals who thrive at bringing people together.

Hub players are the people at the center of the social or business sphere. They're on the move; they excel at connecting themselves and others. Hub players excel at storytelling and typically have a semicircle of folks hanging on their every word. They are not phonies. They are genuinely interested in people; making connections fuels their feelings of happiness. Socializing is their natural state, and the act of meeting people is not an uncomfortable chore or part of a manipulated plan to climb a corporate ladder. At times they may need to recharge, but when they are "on" they know how to work a room, manage a meeting, or direct a dinner conversation. If this sounds like you, congratulations! You have natural networking and relationship-building skills that will serve you well as you navigate your personal and professional relationships. If you are not a hub player or the idea of making small talk at a party makes your skin crawl, don't worry; those skills can be learned and practiced over time.

Hub players usually have an overlap between their personal

and business interests. Their lives are not compartmentalized. Every community is strengthened by business and civic leaders who find it immensely rewarding to knit their personal and business connections into their favorite cause. For example, an art gallery owner might bring friends together to see a new artist. An entrepreneur in the food business builds a clientele who are genuinely his or her friends. They've learned that time management and positive productivity are essential. Hub players are generous with their connections. They don't hoard their contacts, and they are the first to make a warm introduction or a referral. Because of their large networks and secondary circles, hub players are producers, and they get things done. They know how to delegate. They can orchestrate an army of volunteers or interns and reduce project costs by pulling in favors or making trades. In the social space, they curate fantastic dinner parties, are matchmakers, and know how to spark conversations.

Step 9: Hone your connecting skills and learn from hub players.

There are two exercises in this chapter. In Exercise 1, you will practice the name game. In Exercise 2, you will try hub player conversation starters.

Let me introduce you to some hub players who have impacted my own network. What I've learned and encourage you to explore is how working with and knowing hub players strengthen your own social skills and abilities. Cultivating relationships with hub players in your lives is rewarding both professionally and personally. At the end of this chapter, I'll show you what motivates hub players and describe scenarios that create innovative and collaborative bonds, as well as how to spot a hub player if you don't happen to be one yourself.

Learned Connector: All Roads in Los Angeles Lead to Lilly

Lilly Lee's Funnel

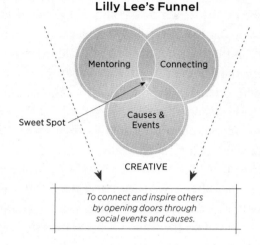

Lilly Lee, a calligrapher and power networker, lives in Los Angeles. Because of Lilly, I now have as many connections in Los Angeles as I do in Minneapolis, New York City, and San Francisco, the three cities where I've lived. She opened the door to finding my way in Hollywood and along the Sunset Strip. It all began when she opened her Rolodex and sprinkled pixie dust on my social life. My journey with Lilly began five years ago at a youth film festival in Seattle called National Film Festival for Talented Youth (NFFTY).

I was asked to speak on a panel at NFFTY. I shared insights into filmmaking and told the audience what type of content we were putting onto the Virgin America in-flight system. Lilly's husband, John, was also on the panel, representing the CW Network. I ran into the couple the next day at breakfast. We talked about children, San Francisco, and films we enjoyed. I would not have predicted that this chance meeting would lead to a friendship filled with barbecues, birthday parties, and benefit events. Nor did I foresee that John and I would work on a business deal two years later when a production company approached Virgin America and pitched us a reality show called *Fly Girls*. It was a risky idea, but our advertising budget was a fraction of our competitors' and our airline needed to build awareness quickly. After running the numbers, we realized that the media value of the show could top $20 million if it made it onto the air. Over the course of the show's development we visited E!, Bravo, the CW Network, and several other networks. It was during that process that I reconnected with John and Lilly.

When Lilly heard I was stopping by the CW, she quickly arranged to see me. She arrived with a butterfly-adorned T-shirt for my daughter and was full of energy and invitations. Soon after, the CW picked up the show. Over the next six months, John and I worked on the terms of the deal, and Lilly and I cemented our friendship. I knew Lilly was a connector when I flew in for one of her parties. She pulled me aside and whispered, "Did you see anyone of interest with a star on their name tag?" Much to my surprise, she had put a secret code onto the calligraphy name tags she had created that was shared only with single girlfriends. A name tag with a star in the corner indicated "single" and one with a heart indicated "married." From one connection with Lilly, I attended a dinner with a man who owned a gold mine, went to a ballet fund-raiser, and filled my own birthday gathering with a cacophony of her friends.

What's interesting is that Lilly wasn't always a hub player. Her husband told her story at a dinner for eighteen she once hosted: "When Lilly and I met twenty years ago, she wasn't a networker. She would ask why I was having lunch with this person or that person. I remember explaining the value of networking to her by singing her the lyrics of the Hawaiian 'Hukilau Song': 'We throw our nets out into the sea, and all the 'ama 'ama [fish] come a-swimming to me.' Now she's a master networker. She does not stop." John also said that Lilly's parents were both Chinese, and they had raised her to view connections as transactions or bargaining chips. Although there are cultural differences to networking around the globe, helping others and being authentic and passionate are traits that are useful anywhere. Over time, Lilly's connecting skills evolved, and she now has an authentic and honest desire to bring people together.

At the dinner, after a three-course meal and five-minute neck massages by a roving masseuse, Lilly called for a round of musical chairs so all attendees could make connections. Lilly constantly reinforces names and encourages dialogue; "Porter, you need to meet [fill in a name]" was the most common phrase of the night. Remembering a person's name not only shows you are listening, it reinforces that you value the conversation. Lilly points out common interests, always provides name tags, and verbally and physically makes an effort to connect people.

Exercise 1: Play the name game.

Following are several ideas to help you remember the names of new people in your network. Try them out at your next event or dinner, and see if any of them work for you.

- Repeat the name just after you've been introduced (e.g., "John, it's nice to meet you").
- Think of a celebrity or another person with a similar name and make a visual link in your head.
- Make a rhyme of the person's name in your head (e.g., "Nancy is fancy").
- Ask the origin of the person's name or if it's a family name.

- Ask if there is a story associated with the person's name.
- Make an association with the first letter of the person's name (e.g., "Craig likes carrots").
- Ask the contact for his or her email address, Twitter handle, or phone number (if appropriate). If you have a smartphone, input the information directly into your contact list, email it to yourself, or write a note on a virtual notepad.
- Focus on the person's face while reciting his or her name, and try to make a mental link in your head.

I've also seen people and businesses send out information prior to events to help attendees remember names. For example, for one high-end conference I attended the host made an event-branded smartphone app that was sent to attendees on flash drives ahead of time. It included photos and details about attendees and their employment, schools, favorite museum, desired superhero trait, contact information, and social media handles. It also allowed attendees to click on a bio and add that person to a "must meet" list. Another tech-savvy way to connect at large events: use networking software distributed via near-field-communication (NFC)-enabled smartphones or flash drives. One brand called Poken allows you to collect reciprocal information with a simple swipe of two devices. Poken technology replaces paper business cards, and data are stored in a timeline that can be downloaded, from an online website, for future reference.

A less technical idea, which is still effective, is to compile a book of facts that can be used for conversation starters and future follow-up. In addition to name and company information, an event book could include attendees' favorite books, movies, road-trip music, or "one thing you can't live without." The low-cost, turnkey version of this idea is to send out a group email prior to an event, with bios or links to personal websites or about.me profiles, which are similar to online résumés. These are all great strategies to encourage dialogue and conversation at events. Exercise two contains some of the greatest hits I've seen by hub players in warming up a room or event and fostering comfortable conversation and new connections.

Exercise 2: Practice hub player conversation starters.

- Start a meal by saying a couple words about each guest.
- Have a "white elephant" gift exchange.
- Have a book exchange.
- Play a game such as "What celebrity do people say you look like?" or "What famous person would you like to meet?"
- Pose a question such as "How do you define happiness?"
- Have an expert (e.g., in wine or art) speak and encourage dialogue.
- Change seats at a planned time during the meal.
- Put fun facts on guests' name tags.
- Put "I will . . ." on name tags and have guests fill in the statement.
- Include an interactive activity (e.g., drum circle, cooking demo, sports activity).
- Host a game night.

An Eco-Minded Hub Player Learns Lessons Living on a Commune

Zem Joaquin is a close friend and a thought leader in the ecological space and, in my experience up to this point, the reigning champion of hub players. My gratitude for our friendship goes very deep, and I'd like to share some of what I've learned from her. I met Zem several years ago when she pitched an environmental content idea to me when I was at Virgin America. I remember being a tad overwhelmed by her during our meeting. She's very focused on her passions, and she knows literally everyone who is anyone. I'm not sure if I was tired, hungry, or just a little off, but I recall thinking, "She's out of my league." I would not have predicted that within two years I would consider her one of my closest friends. The funny thing is, when I asked Zem to recall how she'd felt when meeting me, she said, "I thought you were tough, all business, and I didn't think you liked me."

Here were two successful women with thought bubbles over our heads; mine said, "She's way too cool for me," and hers, "She is one tough chick, I'd better come back with my A game."

Don't let your insecure inner voice hold you back from making new connections. Thankfully, a chance meeting brought Zem and me together a second time when we were both invited to sit at Arianna Huffington's table at a local benefit. A member of the advertising sales team from the *Huffington Post* invited me. And, not surprisingly, Ms. Huffington invited Zem.

At the flower-adorned table, we quickly recalled how we had met months before. On that occasion we talked about personal interests, not just business. As we listened to Ms. Huffington deliver a keynote, we shared that we both enjoyed hiking, have children of similar ages, and are both passionate about media. Soon I found myself on weekly hikes with a friend who has dramatically impacted my social life. Zem is the center of a social hub of eco-minded and tech-focused friends. I've met at least a hundred people through Zem. I've been introduced to companies of interest, attended numerous holiday events, gone on a group vacation, helped at a charity event, and generally felt inspired to be more efficient. People like Zem teach us how expanding our network by just one person can dramatically improve our happiness and productivity levels.

If your inner voice is giving you the negative message "She won't like me" or "She's too cool for me," look at where it stems from. Over time we can reprogram such thoughts of being "less than" and work on developing our relationship-making skills. One of the easiest ways to connect with people is to ask a question or to find a common interest: Tell me more. What types of activities do you enjoy? With Zem, the hiking trail was our common ground. The purity of being outside, talking about our passions, and being 100 percent focused on dialogue paved a way for our strong bond.

I spoke more with Zem about her connecting skills and had some interesting revelations. Zem was raised on a self-described "musical, peace-minded, hippie commune" that had been started by Joan Baez. The community of a couple hundred people was called The Land, and there were nightly musical gatherings and lots of talk about peace and getting along. It was there that the foundation of Zem's connecting skills was established. "I was always running around, making sense of the place," she said. After the commune and with her parents' divorce and frequent moving around, she attended nine schools and three universities. "Connecting was a survival skill," she told me. "Now I can socialize with anyone. I love being the bridge or the connective tissue that brings people together." When I asked Zem why connecting people brings her satisfaction, she replied, "I love knowing other people's stories. I guess I get endorphins learning about people. I like hearing about what makes them happy." She added, "It's also fun to figure out what you have in common. It could be kids or something as simple as liking the same gum, jewelry, or shoes. You look for a connection point and expand the conversation from there."

Learning to Use the Spotlight

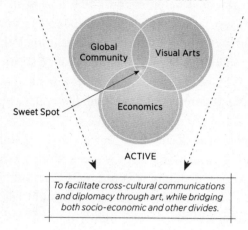

Wendi Norris's Funnel

Global Community

Visual Arts

Economics

Sweet Spot

ACTIVE

To facilitate cross-cultural communications and diplomacy through art, while bridging both socio-economic and other divides.

In 2009, I met another hub player, the art dealer Wendi Norris, when I attended a political fund-raiser at her art gallery. Wendi and I shared an interest in politics, and at the time we were both single moms. Our connection was instantaneous. She was smart, thoughtful, and dynamic. Over the following years we bonded at sporting events, over fine dinners, at dance performances, and at her wedding. "I love bringing people together. It gives me a sense of purpose," she said over coffee. Wendi's networking skills and outgoing personality enabled her to build one of the most successful international contemporary and modern art galleries on the West Coast.

Wendi's personality was tested in 2002 after the dot-com bust. After having laid off her team of forty, she joined the ranks of the unemployed when the company she worked for closed its doors. "I was heartbroken and decided to travel around the world with a backpack. I ended up in Cuba and found myself asking 'What would I do if money didn't matter?'" She knew she had the business skills and drive to start a business. She also had two friends named Kate and Eric who were artists without representation. After careful consideration, she decided to open an art gallery. She wrote a business plan, interviewed thirty people successful in the art world, and started looking for gallery spaces. She hosted her first show at her friends' art studio, sent out invitations to a group in her PalmPilot database of three thousand, and sold her first piece of work by the artists now known as Kate Eric.

"Selling art is a very high-touch business. People often invite you into their homes," Wendi told me. "I visit my clients in their spaces as often as possible, as it helps me to connect with them. I've even traveled to Dubai, dropped off a piece of art, had tea, and flew home to strengthen a relationship. My clients are important, and I do what it takes to build relationships."

Wendi is not only relationship-driven, she is committed to educating and supporting the art community. "I host events, curate panels and roundtables, bring clients to museums for guided tours, and educate the people in our network. My clients like to be around positive, generous people, so I always try to give back."

Wendi believes that any person, young or old and regardless of the first impression they make, needs to be treated with respect when he or she comes into the gallery. "You'd be surprised who the collectors are or even who has the influence over collectors, parents, and friends. I want our space to be accessible to everyone," she said. Her desire to make her gallery accessible to people of all ages also translates to her views on friendships. "I have friends from age twenty to ninety-three. I gain wisdom from my older friends and energy from my younger friends. My cocktail parties are quite a mix," she said with a laugh.

When I asked Wendi about the key to success, she said, "I believe in hard work, education, being magnanimous, and I value people who know what they don't know." She added that she is "one hundred percent fine" surrounding herself with people "smarter" than she is. "I have no problem learning from others or working with smart people, it keeps things exciting."

Wendi has always worked hard. She described the years after college as intensive preparation for building a network and a business. "I used to get to the office before my boss to make coffee," she remembered. "I was the only one without an advanced degree, so I knew I would have to be creative to get assignments. I also used to observe women I respected from afar, watching their communication style, dress, and how they carried themselves." She met one female mentor in the ladies washroom. "Charlene Ledbetter had on an amazing Chanel suit, was trim, and she had an air about her. She was my first mentor," she said. "I had no idea that several years later she'd introduce me over lunch to my next employer. That's networking, not expecting anything out of a relationship. The best way to network is by being authentic."

My friendships with Lilly, Zem, and Wendi didn't grow out of a decision by us to use one another professionally or to burnish our rankings as networkers. Our relationships are strong because we share similar interests and have overlaps in our values and passions. We all believe in giving back and being community-minded. You will find more happiness through your business and social networking efforts when you find and focus on interests and passions you share with new people in your life. When you reach out to a hub player, you'll find the same dynamic that occurs when you meet a new friend, but with exponential levels of energy and feedback. If the two of you share professional interests and embark on a collaboration, get ready to discover new areas of learning and change.

Tune-up Tip: Ask yourself hub player questions.

Below are some questions to keep in mind if you'd like to improve your hub player traits and enhance your connections. Remember to be confident, have a Give Give Get attitude, and focus on your purpose, and your connections will thrive.

1. Am I inquisitive, and do I try to learn about others during conversations?
2. Am I generous about connecting or introducing contacts or friends?
3. Do I actively participate and give back to my contacts as much as I can?
4. Am I always a guest? Or am I often a host?
5. Do I look for connections who share goals or pursuits (e.g., arts, fund-raising)?
6. Am I nurturing relationships with hub players who are geographically close or at least using the same online tools as I am?
7. Am I connecting people for a reason other than financial gain?

You have now finished part II of *Your Network Is Your Net Worth*. You are on your way to developing a transformational attitude and have developed the tools and process to build a values-based team. When building your core team and making connections, remember that the number of degrees of separation between contacts is diminishing, do an audit of your core team to see if you need secondary support to nurture your passions or purpose, set your sights on visiting power pockets, and work on practicing your hub player traits.

Chapter 9: Summary

Step 9: Hone your connecting skills and learn from hub players.

Exercise 1. Play the name game.

Exercise 2. Practice hub player conversation starters.

Tune-up Tip: Ask yourself hub player questions.

Top Tips

1. Practice hub player traits to improve your skills.
2. Remember names to show that you value people.
3. Connect with people based on authentic, honest intentions.
4. Be inquisitive to learn about future projects, connections, and ideas.
5. Use offline and online skills to connect.
6. Remember to have a Give Give Get attitude when connecting with contacts.

Part III

Cultivate Fields of Creativity

Your time is limited, so don't waste it living someone else's
life. . . . Don't let the noise of others' opinions drown out
your own inner voice. And most important, have the courage
to follow your heart and intuition. They somehow already
know what you truly want to become.
—STEVE JOBS

10

Everyone Is a Producer

Create Content, Products, or Services to Share
Your Purpose and Improve Your Reach

Having a mind-set of being a producer will help you focus when generating content or developing products or services to increase your visibility, build your network, or increase your reach.

One morning over tea, my friend Jack described his view on how we can each choose to be a producer or a consumer. "A producer is actively adding to the collective or community, and a consumer is taking away via consumption," he told me. His idea was simple but insightful. "It doesn't matter if you're producing by cooking, blogging, or teaching. The idea is to be giving back to society." He starts each day with ten minutes of thinking. "I don't look at email. I don't read Yahoo! news, I just sit and think about concepts, ideas, write a blog, or do something where I'm producing rather than consuming." Jack's routine demonstrates the mind-set you need to have to bring your passions and purpose to the world in a productive way.

In this chapter, I will talk a lot about content creation. However, your productive output should be based on your passions and purpose. For example, if you love technology, your output may be developing or creating apps. If you are passionate about education, your output might include developing sharable teaching tools. If one of your passions is family, you might offer babysitting services to a family member in need. The goal of being a producer is to add value to the collective good based on your passions and purpose. As Joseph Campbell stated in *The Power of Myth*, "My general formula for my students is 'Follow your bliss.' Find where it is, and don't be afraid to follow it." Tom Stone, a violinist in the Cypress Quartet, also shared thoughts on this subject: "When I'm creating music, often time stops. I can practice for hours and hours without realizing time has passed."

As a producer, you should actively seek to create content, products, or services that support your passions. When you do so, those activities will often result in creative enjoyment, sharable assets, and possibly financial gain. The more you enjoy your producing process, the easier it will be for you to share your output and excitement with others. In this chapter, I'll share examples of people who are actively producing content or creating products to build their networks, improve their credibility, and in some cases develop income streams.

In recent years, I've met numerous people who have mastered the art of producing, both in the content world and in their offline lives. The most successful have a focused purpose and plan and have figured out how to utilize technology to spread their messages and increase their reach. To chat about this, I met Shira Lazar, a self-described "media empress," at a coffee shop in Venice Beach to hear how she uses new media to network and build her career as a Web show host.

Step 10: Create content, products, or services to share your purpose.

In this chapter, you'll do three exercises. In Exercise 1, you'll assess your desire to be a producer to develop content, products, or services. Exercise 2 provides you with guidance to perform an online audit of your personal brand.

Going Digital: A Media Empress Who Isn't Afraid to Hustle

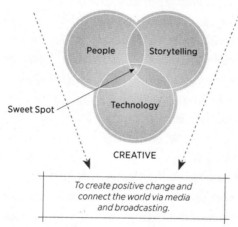

Shira Lazar's Funnel

People

Storytelling

Technology

Sweet Spot

CREATIVE

To create positive change and connect the world via media and broadcasting.

Ms. Lazar graduated from college in 2004 and wanted to get on-air experience but didn't want to wait forever to land a cable or network gig. A young "aspiring Katie Couric," she skipped the traditional route to becoming a television journalist and unleashed the power of the Web via her weekly online show What's Trending. Through hard work and her infectious entrepreneurial spirit, Shira and her business partner, Damon Berger, have hundreds of thousands of fans on social media and have scored Web interviews with Sir Richard Branson, Drew Carey, Snoop Dogg, Mark Cuban, Tony Hsieh, and will.i.am.

"I tend to relate to hip-hop artists, as we share the same hustle and aren't afraid to self-promote to get what we want and live the dream," she told me. Before Shira launched her show, she built a promotional reel by taking hosting gigs at red-carpet events and doing nonstop networking. "I'd take any job to get my foot in the door," she said with a smile. Eventually, Shira and her partner scored a seven-figure deal with CBS. "It was exciting, but we never stopped to celebrate, there was too much to do," she said. After several months, their contract was abruptly dropped after a junior staffer at What's Trending erroneously reported on their Twitter account that Steve Jobs had died based on false news overheard in the newsroom. A frenzy started in the press as the tweet was picked up around the globe. Ms. Lazar apologized for the error, but the contract with CBS was canceled.

"I was devastated, but we called people in our network, raised money, and decided to self-fund. I knew that hard work and great content would overpower the negative publicity," she said. "What's Trending is our baby, I blog all day and embrace the start-up mentality rather than fight it. Being independent is a way to survive as you create your own fan base, and you don't have to rely on partners. It's the new model. Troubleshooting, getting over obstacles, and building my business have made me stronger."

After the CBS deal folded, Shira and Damon went on to win four International Academy of Web Television awards and secured distribution deals with YouTube, Mashable, Ustream, Blip, and others. She noted, "It's a time of new business models, and whoever is hungry and creates good content will be pioneers of the new media age."

Shira's success is due in part to her determination to relentlessly pursue followers for her network. "I have no shame adding people on Facebook, and I'm very good at researching how people are connected. I work every angle to get a meeting or book an interview," she said. "There's usually only one degree of separation between people. If I find a common connection, I'll ask them to vouch for me that I always show people in their best light. I also make interviews worth the time and repurpose content on several other sites for added reach," she added with a smile.

Her advice for others? Keep learning, stay humble, develop sincere relationships, contribute as much as you can, and remember that successful people don't wait for opportunities—they create them.

Tune-up Tip: Reframe blogging as advocating your passions.

When creating content, I recommend reframing your efforts as advocating your passions. Share about what you love, what you are passionate about, and you are likely to have greater success. Use your passions and purpose as a filter for your content, products, or services.

One Man's Passion: I Can't Believe I Get Paid to Do This

Om Malik has also leveraged new media to build an audience, a brand, and a business. In the early 1990s, Om wanted a job as a reporter at Forbes.com and sent fax after fax and made call after call to the editor. "I don't know how to take no for an answer. I'm an immigrant. I don't have anyone looking out for me. If I need something, I figure it out and go get it." His persistence worked; he was hired. Today he continues to write about technology and the Internet but now has a company that employs "about fifty people," and his blog, GigaOM, has over 6 million unique visitors a month. Mr. Malik is successful because of his laserlike focus on the space. He also prefers to write about ideas: "I don't care who people are dating." It is also apparent that he puts relationships first: "There are quite a few people in the Valley that I have email relationships with, we share ideas, but often our conversations are confidential." Building trust is one reason Mr. Malik has been given access and story leads.

Mr. Malik has assembled a team of like-minded writers so he can curate more content and have more ideas and points of view included on GigaOM. Furthermore, stories on the site have social media integration so articles can be tweeted, shared, and posted. Over the years, Mr. Malik's company has also expanded its offerings to include events and research that increase the reach and ability of his team to be experts in the technology space. "We've gone from one voice to a lot of like-minded voices. We're like bandmates, we're similar but different and all part of the same rhythm. Some of the people who work with us will be massive. I hope they'll be so amazing that they will outshadow everyone. David Churbuck at Forbes.com made me a better writer and a better person. It's my job to make sure my team is getting that same opportunity. What else is there?"

Mr. Malik also told me that a heart attack in 2007 caused him to "look at things a bit differently." He gave up his addictions and put cigars and cigarettes aside. "Addiction is really more mental than physical. It takes three days to beat the nicotine fix. What you have to give up is the crutch it's associated with. Maybe you don't think you're cool without the cigarette or you can't talk to the girl without the smoke, but that's all in your head." He added, "When I drank it was nonsense, it didn't alleviate stress."

One addiction he can't toss aside is his passion for work, reading, and writing. He typically works eighteen-hour days, and that's what makes him happy. "The days I don't write or talk to interesting people are the days I'm unhappy. If I start and end my day with questions, it's a home run," he said. "I can't believe I get paid to write and interview interesting people. That's the great thing about America; you get paid to do what you love. At the end of the day, the container is not very important, it's the ideas that will live on." He smiled.

Shira, Damon, and Om are producing or curating new, well-researched content that is highly engaging to build their businesses and personal brands, but producing content or blogging can also be used to nurture and maintain personal relationships and to help create positive change. Meet Liz Rowan, a blogger from Vancouver, Washington.

A Young Woman's Fight Against Cancer: "Can't Stop Living"

Liz Rowan, a twenty-one-year-old woman fighting leukemia, is close to my heart. When Liz and her twin sister, Julia, were four, their mother, Beth, was featured in a documentary I coproduced about breast cancer survivors. Their mother passed away when the twins were six, and Liz explained, "I watch the documentary when I can't remember her voice. I go back to it for comfort and like the scene of her making peanut butter sandwiches." At age sixteen, Liz had her first bout of cancer. At eighteen, Liz tattooed a phrase her mom said in the film, "Can't stop living" on her torso. By twenty, she had battled cancer four times, and her urge to share her story grew. She found me via Twitter.

"I've always loved writing, and my blog has also helped me find other young people with cancer. My friends are great, but sometimes it is hard to relate to them. Sharing with other young people who have cancer somehow makes things easier," she explained. Her blog taps the sharing capabilities of social media so participants can share their experiences with and insights into treatments and cancer protocols. Her dad, Rod, said, "When you have a shared thread, you don't have to explain drug A or drug B, and you can emotionally understand each other." The family also uses the blog to keep people updated, "so our evenings aren't overrun with phone calls."

Rod, who is a fireman, said, "The other day I was in the back of an ambulance racing to the hospital at ninety miles per hour, holding an oxygen mask to a woman's face so she could breathe. For a total stranger, I'm able to hold her in this world, yet for my own daughter I'm only able to nestle her into the crook of my shoulder and tell her she is loved." He added, "I want people to know how amazing Elizabeth is, and our story puts life into perspective. When we share, people take action. They donate blood, maybe give a couple of bucks to a homeless man, and they become more motivated." Liz added that she tries to keep her blog focused on "me and my journey," but she does include bits about her family such as "my brother being deployed." Liz would like to give a voice to young people with cancer. "It is hard to be sixteen or twenty-one and have cancer. When I lost my hair, people treated me differently and didn't know how to act. It was like I was a delicate flower that nobody wanted to pick. I also blog to connect with people, because when I'm in the hospital it feels like I'm alone in a hole in the ground. I don't want anyone else to feel that loneliness." Liz wrote in her blog, "It's interesting what cancer brings out in people. I feel like people are ready to put me in the ground. I am not going down without a fight. I am not dead yet. I will fight until my heart stops beating. I will not give up to this disease."

Recently, an article on Liz appeared in a local newspaper, and an elderly man read the story and emailed her, "Keep your head up, you're so strong and don't worry about your future husband. He won't see your scars. My wife has MS and I still love her the same." Liz smiled. "The email touched my heart. I know someday a boy will come along. The email made me happy."

An important aspect of being a producer is to focus your tone and to create content, products, or services that support your passions. Liz writes about her struggle with cancer, and Om writes about technology and digital trends. Though the subject matter couldn't be more different, both are effective producers because their content is authentic and reflects their in-depth knowledge of the subjects. Before launching or posting any content, remember to focus your message around your passions and purpose and use your authentic tone of voice.

In some cases, the act of producing is not blogging but the act of making physical products or providing services. For example, Lauren Van Horn, a lawyer turned entrepreneur, was looking for an aesthetically pleasing eyeglass stand to give to her husband for his birthday. She posted a request on Zaarly, a site that helps people connect to buy and sell services, and described her vision. Tobi Adamolekun, a designer and architect, responded to the request and made the eyeglass stand. The result was so successful that the duo started a company called Bushakan to sell the product. Technology brought the pair together, but a physical product was the basis of their connection and output.

Or consider Becky Reese (chapter 14); she is passionate about health and wellness and is producing a fitness line for women sized 10 to 18. Because of changes in technology, the barriers to producing, connecting, selling, and collaborating with others have been greatly reduced. During a recent trip to a flea market, because of advances in technology, an independent jeweler was able to show and sell her wares to me and charge my credit card with a simple swipe of Square, an electronic payment service that allows credit cards to be accepted through mobile phones. This advance may appear small, but even small changes to the commerce ecosystem ultimately impact how we network, connect, and trade or sell products and services.

Because numerous connections are made over the Internet, it's important to understand that what you produce and how you connect makes an impression on others and will have a direct impact on your ability to build and nurture your network. Stef Michaels, or @adventuregirl, whom you met in chapter 5, has built an online brand around travel. Several years ago, Ms. Michaels learned about the power of her voice, or in this case 140 characters, after several of her tweets upset some followers. She told me that Michael Jackson had on died her birthday. "I was watching Michael's memorial telecast and Lionel Richie was singing a very, very long song. I posted a tweet that said, 'Can't we just move on, could he pick a different song?'" She wasn't trying to be disrespectful, but she lost a number of followers on Twitter. "Now I frame it right or zip it. I stay away from religion, politics, and sexual issues, as those topics have nothing to do with my brand." She added, "In today's age everyone has an opinion, but we need to be responsible. Words can hurt. Or words can help. I try to post words that help."

Your productive output and blogs need to be framed appropriately, as messages can go viral quickly. For example, Mr. Malik posted on his blog that he was deleting his account from one of the major social media networks because of "spam and too many emails." He told me, "Some people only read the headline and made assumptions about the state of the company. Soon I had an email from the CEO asking why I wrote the piece. I would never want to take down a company. I know how hard people work. You have to be careful what messages you put out there—especially the headlines."

Become an Expert: Articles, Awards, and Associations

Producing content about your passions, product, or services and receiving relevant awards can also raise your profile as an expert in your industry and open the door to new contacts and new revenue opportunities. When I left my post at Virgin America, I made a conscious effort to raise my profile by writing and producing content so I could share my insights with others.

Before approaching publications, I wrote a sample post titled "Serendipity in the Sky: Conversations with 4C" that detailed stories and lessons I had learned chatting with random people on airplanes. With a draft in hand, I emailed a sales representative I knew at the *Huffington Post* and asked for a warm introduction to an editor. With the introduction, I sent in a finely crafted email with the sample post. I used a similar process to connect with contacts at *Advertising Age*. After a quick back-and-forth, both editors agreed that I could blog, or produce, for them on a regular basis. This is where it gets tricky. I agreed to write content and was not hired as an on-staff writer. So often producing is a bit like sweat equity: you need to make sure you can glean a return in ways that are not directly deposited in your bank account. For me, the exposure kept my name in the forefront, and I included in my bio that I do public speaking. With every post, I gained Twitter followers and usually received a speaking engagement inquiry, which does generate income. So the return on investment wasn't a direct payment from a publication but came quickly via a larger network and reach and more consulting opportunities. For example, consider the duo that started the wooden eyeglass stand company. To gain exposure, they could pitch a behind-the-scenes video or how-to story on the process they use to make their product. That exposure, in turn, would help them build their network and potentially increase their sales.

Partnering with or blogging for publications with built-in reach is a faster way to find an audience than starting from ground zero with your own blog or website. In my case, I instantly had posts that were retweeted up to seven hundred times on *Advertising Age*, and my stories reached people around the globe. Within a year, I had companies offering me exclusive stories and people sending me press releases about products, and I secured a reputation as a writer in the marketing and digital communities. If you do start writing for a publication, interviewing people for stories is a great way to make new contacts and learn about your industry. If appropriate, consider profiles and question-and-answer formats.

A way to extend the reach of your content is to form an informal alliance with appropriate contacts and ask for retweets. For example, several writers from *Fast Company*, CNET, and *Forbes* often email me and ask me to post or tweet out links to new articles. I gladly post their content if their articles are in line with my passions and purpose. However, if a contact asked me to retweet a blog on mixed drinks or tips to put a baby to sleep, I would decline, as the content does not support my passions or purpose. So consider looking for like-minded bloggers and form an informal group and help each other as much as possible with retweets and Follow Friday (#FF) posts and by sharing content.

Tune-up Tip: Learn the blogging basics.

A good length to consider is six hundred words. Attention spans have decreased and multitasking has increased, so keep your content short and concise. Make your headline memorable but not clichéd. Enable social sharing on all posts and post not only on your blog but also on your social media channels. Include your Twitter handle and URL in your byline. Consider blogs with easy-to-digest "top tips" lists or question-and-answer formats.

Another tip for building your online profile is to review content (e.g., photos, videos) that you have available for posting. For example, during the course of writing this book, I recorded the stories of numerous people via iPhone recordings. Some of the interviews are so interesting that I've gathered friends around my kitchen table and we've listened to the files like an old-world radio program. My coffeemates were glued to the stories. Why not tweet out a clip from an interview with the violinist Tom Stone or a sound byte from Larry Baer, the CEO of the San Francisco Giants? So one step to building your online brand or blog is to take photos, start documenting, and create a library of the steps you are taking to live your passions and purpose.

You can also raise your profile by developing your reputation as an expert and to be recognized within your industry or peer group by accumulating industry awards or speaking at events. I asked Ali Brown, the entrepreneurial coach, about how she had raised her profile, and she said with a laugh, "I wanted to win some awards, so I went online and googled 'women entrepreneur awards' and filled out applications for awards that looked good. It took some time, and my company was audited for several entries, but like Woody Allen said, 'Eighty percent of success is just showing up' or in this case filling out the applications."

I also have been fortunate to win several industry awards. There is one downside to consider; often organizations presenting the award expect the recipient to fill a table by selling seats to the luncheon or gala where it is offered. At one point, I had to decline an award since I had recently tapped my network for ticket sales to a previous banquet. I felt that asking for seat sales so soon thereafter would be inappropriate. So enthusiasts beware; a get might actually be an undercover give.

Becoming an Industry Expert:
A Foundation for Global Adventures

Another way to add luster to your professional brand or be a producer with your own superiors and peers is to establish a new industry resource or practice. In 2005, Heather LeFevre, a strategic planner in the advertising business, launched a salary survey on planners. In 2005, 133 people responded to her survey. By 2011, her sample size had grown to 2,113 people, and questionnaires were filled out around the globe. She used her industry's own tools to help her peers make sure the playing field is level.

Ms. LeFevre told me, "I started doing the survey because it was time for my performance evaluation and I wanted to make sure I was fairly compensated. I got a raise and a promotion that year—as did many of the people who took the survey—so I kept doing it. Now I'm kind of famous in my industry. I can go to any city, and planners are happy to meet with me." She has also been invited to speak at conferences around the world, including in Brazil, Poland, and Romania. Her willingness to devote the work and time to provide vital insights to her peers allowed her to build a robust, diversified network and ultimately helped her create long-lasting connections and experiences.

Exercise 1: Assess your desire and resources to produce content, products, and/or services to build your reach and profile.

1. Revisit your goals and purpose.
2. Define who you are trying to reach.
3. Consider your tone and needs.
4. Consider your producing abilities: products, services, and/or content.
5. Use technology to extend your reach to connect with others.
6. Identify two or three publications for potential reach/coverage.

Turning a Hobby into a Purpose: Blending Offline DIY and Online Technology

One person who has used the power of technology to build her brand and her network is Brit Morin. Recently, Ms. Morin left her post as product marketing manager at Google and decided to start her own company, Brit + Co., that brings crafting and technology to the masses. "I was planning my wedding, and I joined TechShop, a three-level members-only warehouse in San Francisco where you can use equipment from woodworking machines and wood saws to sewing machines and vinyl cutters to make crafts. It's like a gym but for making things," she explained. Surrounded by creative people, she discovered her true passion. "I became very immersed in it all," she said with a smile. Her discovery ultimately led her to create her new company, which "teaches the digital generation savvy shortcuts for their everyday lives, and it's all centered around technology, innovation, and creating." She said, "I saw the opportunity to teach and help people around the world to live better lives, and I took it."

For Ms. Morin the worlds of offline and online technology intersect in numerous ways. She uses social media "every day and all day" and is often found on Google +, YouTube, Twitter, Tumblr, Facebook, Pinterest, or StumbleUpon. Around the Web, Ms. Morin has more than 2 million followers. "Social is time-consuming, but when growing a brand it's one of the most effective tools, as you have a dialogue with users. Many brands and companies realize SEO [search engine optimization] isn't the only way to play the game to build Web traffic." She noted, "Email lists are also important, but there are so many ways for people to interact with you. If they like you, they can bookmark your site or download your app to their iPad or iPhone.

"It's true that you need to find the thing that you love to do and learn how to make money at it," she added. Even before she launched her business, she produced content about new ideas and technology and had started to build a following. "I've been doing this my whole life. When I was young, I was the first to have new gadgets, I had a lemonade stand, and I was the top Girl Scout cookie seller numerous years in a row. This is my purpose. The fact that crafting and making things is now my business only makes it more exciting." Ms. Morin's passion and interests have always been consistent, but now she's found a way to use technology to increase her reach and monetize her core interests.

She added, "I remember sitting on my dad's knee when I was nine. He said, 'You can do anything you want in this life.' It always stuck out to me. So I have ambitions to be a household name, and I'm going to make that happen." Her advice to others is to "find a niche that hasn't been filled, be authentic, differentiate from the masses, be passionate, and don't let your life be wasted."

Tune-up Tip: Develop digital reach—building strategies.

There are numerous books on building website traffic, but questions to ask yourself or your webmaster or team include:

- Have I integrated social sharing into my site, blog, and emails?
- Have I considered how content and keywords can help improve search engine optimization?
- Can I repurpose my content on sites with added reach?
- Are there like-minded bloggers whom I can partner with to build cross-blog traffic?
- Are there backlinks or inbound links that can be added to my site for increased traffic?
- Have I submitted my website to the major search engines and Internet directories? (To do so, locate instructions on each site,

Google, Yahoo!, Bing, Foursquare, Twitter, Citysearch, etc., and
submit several times a year.)

If creating products and services, writing articles, or applying
for awards is daunting, one way to move forward is by producing
with actions that require only small investments of time. For example, if you love travel, you can pin your favorite travel images
on Pinterest. Or, if you're passionate about food, start posting
your favorite food images on your Instagram account.

I spoke with Nish Nadaraja, a former brand marketing director at Yelp, a site that hosts consumer-generated reviews of
businesses. "You don't need to be a food critic anymore to have
an opinion on food," Mr. Nadaraja said. "People have a desire
to be seen and heard, and posting reviews is one way to get your
opinion in the marketplace." He told me that one Yelper had
monetized his efforts when he was hired by the *San Francisco
Chronicle* to write food reviews. For others, Yelp provides a place
to network and meet others with similar interests. Yelp Elite
Squad members, or heavy Yelp users, are invited to VIP events,
bar openings, and parties. Mr. Nadaraja added, "I've made lots of
great friends because of Yelp. Based on reviews, you can tell if you
have similar interests or like the same food or music as someone.
And yes, there have been some weddings that have resulted from
Yelpers meeting." He laughed and added, "You can read reviews
and message people to be part of something or to fill that need
for community," he said. As in traditional networking, he urges
people not to ask for too many favors too soon and be mindful
of their communication tone. "Try to be flattering, not demand-
ing, try to sound like a fan, but don't come off as too needy." Mr.
Nadaraja is particularly optimistic about the options technology
offers for communicating your message or vision. "Emotion can
be transferred over the superhighway," he said. "By attaching a

video or a photo, you can really make an impact. We've moved past simple email and can send more than words to open a door or make an impression."

Impressions are made both online and offline, so do a Google search to see what impression you are making.

Exercise 2: Do an audit of your online personal brand with Google.

Search Google for photos, videos, and Web hits, and see what you find. What impression or story do the images and content create? One way to add content and images to your search quickly is by posting on Google +, as content is quickly integrated into search inquiries.

Offline Impressions Matter Too: Reinforce Your Passions and Purpose

After you've reviewed your online results, review how your on-line and offline personas mesh with your passions and purpose. I've been in marketing for more than twenty years, and it is true that first impressions matter. But today your intellect, interests, and authentic self are a faster route to success than a designer suit or $200 highlights. Your strongest safety nets are your skills and network. The most important aspect of building your persona is having a barrier-breaking attitude and constantly assessing what's holding you back and how you can improve.

Remember, your persona is more about your head and your attitude than the car you're driving or your earrings. It's about your conversations, your ideas, your thoughts, and how you inter-act with the world. It's also about being authentic. For example, consider Zem Joaquin (chapter 9), who is a thought leader in the ecological space. Because of her passions and purpose, her wardrobe selections are typically manufactured with a green or organic process that doesn't damage the environment. Zem drives a hybrid, and she has solar panels installed on the roof of her home. What impression would she make if she drove a Range Rover or a Hummer?

Nick Graham, the founder of Joe Boxer, is another example of a person who has created a strong personal brand. Nick is on the cusp of every trend, and his taste for fashion and creativity is reflected in his bright scarves, ascots, striped suits, and Converse All Star shoes. Ido Leffler, of the skin care company Yes To Carrots, is often seen wearing bright orange. You'll also see him in orange in press photos and his social media pictures, and the color is splashed throughout his home and corporate office. He shared the story behind his commitment to the color orange. "I flew from Israel to Deerfield, Illinois, to have what was supposed to be a thirty-minute meeting. I had on a bright orange tie. The buyer from Walgreens walked up to me and stuck out her hand, and I pushed it aside and said, 'In Israel we kiss on each cheek.' The meeting went on for three hours, and we talked about life, business, and ended up going from a 16-store to a 5,800-store deal. It was life-changing." Mr. Leffler has worn orange every working day since, for six years, "for good luck and to remember where we came from. And it makes people happy." The day we chatted, he had orange trim on his shoes, an orange belt, an orange T-shirt under a black pullover, an orange bracelet from Kenya, an orange iPhone cover, and an orange wallet.

Another way to be memorable in meetings is to reinforce your name. George Kliavkoff, an EVP at Hearst Entertainment, would accept positions at his last three companies only if his employment contract clearly stated that they would break the corporate naming protocol and he could be referred to as George K and georgek@ in email. He likes his last name but feels it's too hard to remember. When I met him for lunch, our reservation was of course listed under George K.

I myself have changed my name and use my middle name as my first name. If you knew me in high school, I was Polly Gale. No offense to people named Polly, but it's hard for me even to type. It never felt right. In my early twenties, I was promoted from account executive to senior account executive, and the company I was with was going to print me new business cards. "Stop the press, I'm switching to Porter, my middle name," I told the office manager. People thought I was crazy, but in less than a year, everyone including my eighty-something grandmother made the switch. Now not a day goes by when a new acquaintance doesn't point out the uniqueness of my name. I've heard "I love your name" more times than I could possibly count.

Tune-up Tip: Be aware of the impact of profanity on your persona.

Unless you're a stand-up comedian, F-bombs never help your personal brand. Think twice before you throw a four-letter word into your conversations or presentations.

I fear some of you are saying by now, "I have no interest in making stuff, blogging, or using social media, and I wouldn't be caught dead wearing orange." But remember that having the mind-set of a producer goes deeper than just using online tools or reinforcing your name or your persona. Producing or adding to the greater collective can manifest itself in mentoring, public speaking, or giving back. Producing is a mind-set of giving and adding rather than taking. It's a state of mind and a conscious focus of creating output that is based on your passions and purpose. Producing may involve gathering associates for a potluck, creating a community garden, or hosting a benefit event. Create your own plan of action based on your passions and purpose, and always consider if technology can help you increase your reach, spread your message, or help you nurture your network.

Chapter 10: Summary

Step 10: Create content, products, or services to share your purpose.

Tune-up Tip: Reframe blogging as advocating your passions.

Tune-up Tip: Learn the blogging basics.

Exercise 1. Assess your desire and resources to produce content, products, and/or services to build your reach and profile.

Tune-up Tip: Develop digital reach—building strategies.

Exercise 2. Do an audit of your online personal brand with Google.

Tune-up Tip: Be aware of the impact of profanity on your persona.

Top Tips

1. Decide if you are a producer or a consumer.
2. Be productive and hustle.
3. Blog about what you know.
4. Increase your visibility with awards and judging opportunities.
5. Remember to filter words as needed online.
6. Form informal alliances with like-minded bloggers.
7. Make sure your offline persona matches your passions and purpose.

Reaching Critical Mass

Harness Influencers, Partners, and Groups to Accelerate
Positive Change and Growth

Reaching critical mass can be accelerated by connecting with
core influencers, exploring partnerships, and unleashing the
power of groups. Use your passions and purpose as a filter to
focus your connecting efforts and achieve your goals.

Building your audience and the reach of your personal brand
or message online takes effort, but the returns can be multifold.
Classic brand-building techniques such as creating partnerships,
identifying key influencers, combining press and social media,
among others, can be used to target your message, network, and
build a following.

Step 11: Develop partnerships to extend your reach.

In this chapter there are two exercises. In Exercise 1, you will
look for nonblogging ways to extend your reach. In Exercise 2,
you will identify potential partner groups.

A Radio Executive Turns to Social Media: A Country Star Is Born

Jessica Northey's Funnel

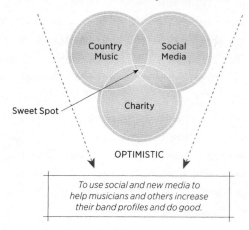

Jessica Northey, who has more than 465,000 followers, is a virtual friend I met on Twitter. She understands the value of focusing on your passions, targeting your message, and having an authentic voice. Jessica's love of media started in college. She had half a dozen jobs, including as a receptionist at a radio station, an on-air traffic reporter, and a nanny for a radio station owner. Over time, she moved into broadcast sales to build her income. Around 2004, she raised her hand in a station sales meeting and offered to "figure out how to monetize Myspace." Concurrently, her roommate had just graduated from the University of Notre Dame Law School and was "raving about The Facebook." Soon Ms. Northey became an early adopter of social media and decided to start a company in the space. "I loved mobile and decided technology was the future. I started by selling SMS or text messaging, but then Twitter came around and I realized I could show companies how to use it without spending $2,000 a month on a 555 number and five to six cents a text. Immediately,

I was hooked." She added, "I try to stay two steps ahead. Also, everything I learned in radio helps. I know I have to find the right people, talk in the right voice, and be online at the right time."

Ms. Northey is now a leading voice in the country music community, and she spends time teaching musicians and others how to build their online brands. The lessons here are familiar but oh, so important: know your audience and give them relatable, engaging, fresh content. "If you're a good-looking twenty-five-year-old male singer, you'll probably appeal to a sixteen-to-twenty-four core audience with mommy cougars as your secondary audience. If you want soccer moms, they're checking Facebook after *The View*, and you should be too. If you want nightclub folks, don't expect to find them online at eight A.M., they're sleeping." Ms. Northey feels strongly that you need to set goals, have a great photo, not just a logo, on social sites, and talk about your passions. "You need to be authentic and find your voice. I talk about country music, the Dallas Cowboys, Nascar, and my dog. If you love Betty Boop bobbleheads you should talk about that. Talk about what you love, and focus on your niche."

Ms. Northey told me, "My first year wasn't easy, especially at Christmastime, when I had nonexistent presents under an invisible tree, but then I hit a turning point. I was invited to speak at conferences, was featured in a book, and suddenly my heroes started following me. I got goose bumps and did a happy dance when I realized I was the first person that Merle Haggard followed and retweeted." Ms. Northey feels her success happened because she is authentic and passionate and works hard. "There is room for everyone, so don't give up," she said. To build her community, she hosts an online chat called #CMchat once a week, helps others, tries not to turn down charity requests, never swears, invites people into dialogue rather than telling them what to do, and sticks to her passions. She also follows individuals on

Twitter who follow people with bios or profiles similar to hers, as she feels "they tend to be the most engaged, create dialogue, and become your fans. When you start building your online community, it is a confidence builder. I'm thrilled when people retweet my content or chat with me about country music. I value the people in my network, and they value me."

The power of critical mass and reach can also be harnessed to help solve local and world problems, create change, and spread messages faster and more efficiently than ever before. Spreading a message on a mass scale is no longer reserved for companies buying expensive ads on prime-time specials. Connections and conversations are moving from Facebook and Twitter pages to real-time events, meet-ups, and flash mobs. For example, the power of online reach dramatically impacted the life of Amit Gupta, the founder of Photojojo, who lives in New York City.

Leveraging Social Media to Find a Needle in a Haystack

Late in September 2011, Mr. Gupta had been feeling weak for more than a month. He thought maybe he had mononucleosis, but he was wrong. One weekend, he ran a high fever and ended up having his wisdom teeth pulled after his dentist found they were infected. "A week after getting my teeth pulled, I was so tired I went to see my doctor. He couldn't find anything wrong but ordered blood tests and sent me home. I went to the lobby, sat down, and was so lethargic I couldn't image how I would make it three blocks to my apartment." The next day his doctor called and gave him the grim news: the blood tests showed he had acute leukemia and needed to start treatment immediately. He called his dad, and they agreed he would go home to Connecticut for treatment. To get the okay to travel, he had to go in for blood transfusions and antibiotics that night. He finished the transfusions at 4 A.M. and took the next plane home. Between phone calls to family and friends, he spent time on Google and found he had a fast-growing cancer, "if I didn't do something I'd be dead in two or three weeks."

Mr. Gupta soon learned he would need a bone marrow transplant, but finding the perfect bone marrow match would be a challenge. Amit is Indian, or of South Asian descent, a population that is dramatically underrepresented in existing bone marrow registries. The chances of finding a perfect or 10/10 match were 1 in 20,000. All this came to light when some of Amit's friends were visiting him from New York City. "My friend Tony started a bone marrow drive in New York, and others started one in San Francisco. People started tweeting and posting. I thought it would blow over in a day or two, but it didn't; my friends kept spreading the word and created a website and launched a campaign across the country, calling temples, South Asian student groups, colleges, putting listings on Facebook, posting on Tumblr and more," he told me.

Mr. Gupta's friends not only mobilized a drive to help find a match; their efforts also gave him a sense of purpose and a goal. "When I first went to the hospital, I was feeling pretty sorry for myself. I was crestfallen and thinking about how dramatically this had shortened my life. People banding together pulled me out of a funk, and instead of feeling sorry for myself I had a mission to help coordinate drives and spread the message."

Mr. Gupta feels the effort would not have been successful without Facebook, Tumblr, and Twitter. "It would have taken a year to spread the word in the past. Digital tools made it easy and quick to do all of this," he said. Because of the efforts of a group he described as "my friends, friends of my friends, and strangers I'll never meet," two potential 10/10 matches were found from the drives that were mobilized in his honor. "It was pretty amazing that we found a match. I'm now thirty-two days out from transplant. The first year is critical. I can't go outside without a mask, and I can't eat outside food; it's kind of like being under house arrest. I'm grateful for all the help and thankful to all of you who helped someone you didn't know."

Mr. Gupta's advice for others who may be facing a similar situation is to have a concrete goal and make your story as relatable as possible. "Many people said they could see themselves in my story, and I think that's one reason they wanted to help. I was so touched and surprised by how much people helped me. In short, my friends and strangers saved my life," he said.

Unleashing the power of online reach generated more than 20 million tweets about Mr. Gupta. The power of one man's story and the use of social media mobilized communities, sparked press articles, and spread hope and awareness around the globe. I originally heard about Mr. Gupta when I had dinner with several inspiring female friends. One of the women, a professor at Stanford University named Jennifer Aaker, had started an effort to increase sign-ups on the Be The Match registry to help individuals like Mr. Gupta. She told me about Mr. Gupta, and we decided to put our skills together to see if we could raise awareness of his plight. With the professor, I cowrote several stories about Mr. Gupta. One strategy we found that was successful was blending press or blogs with online social media techniques. For example, for *Advertising Age* we cowrote a story titled "Can Social Media Save Amit Gupta?" That one piece had 570 retweets on Twitter, 298 likes on Facebook, and 208 shares on LinkedIn. In addition, when the story went live, several people spreading the word on Mr. Gupta's behalf asked heavy social media users to retweet the story. The piece was republished on Beth Kanter's blog and posted on the *Huffington Post* and on several other websites. Repurposing content, accelerating reach via key digital influencers, and asking publications to tweet and post from their social accounts is a very powerful way to create change and spread messages.

I asked the CEO of Twitter, Dick Costolo, how he felt about Mr. Gupta's story, and his eyes filled with emotion. "It's amazing; one of the easy parts of this job is being able to articulate the motivation of why we have to be successful. From the ridiculous to the sublime, we get emails, letters, and gifts from around the world saying 'Twitter has changed my life.'" Mr. Costolo told me he has heard stories from people in the revolution in Tunisia to women in Egypt who say that social media allowed them to organize in ways they couldn't before to take back their governments. He added, "It's overwhelming, it's just extraordinary. Twitter has also eradicated the psychological status barriers that exist between us." He told me, "The Oklahoma State fraternity guys aren't going to call NBA star Kevin Durant on his cell phone and say, 'Come play flag football with us.' That's not going to happen, but it did on Twitter. The president of Rwanda will respond to tweets, but you'd be hard pressed to go to the steps of the presidential palace and have a conversation with him. Twitter has changed how we get things done and how we connect with people, whether it's a CEO, an investor, or a football player."

Exercise 1: Identify ways other than blogging to extend your reach.

Express your passions or purpose outside of the blogosphere to extend your reach, credibility, and potential network. For example, you could:

- Write industry articles, research, or white papers.
- Make yourself available for press interviews.
- Teach a class.

- Volunteer at a relevant organization.
- Start a fund-raising effort.
- Provide products or services to events and organizations.

Tune-up Tip: Consider Change.org and Kickstarter as potential online platforms to spread your ideas or message or to raise funds.

One way to build a network is to tap into existing communities that may share or support your interests. Look for online platforms, like Change.org or Kickstarter, that can help you bring your message to the masses.

Take This Lollipop: Halloween Video Opens Doors

Another passion project I watched go viral was a spooky video called "Take This Lollipop," which was released before Halloween last year by director Jason Zada. I met Jason where I meet a lot of friends, sitting in seat 4C on Virgin America. Because we chatted on the plane, Jason and I later connected on Facebook. As a result, I see his posts regularly. Everything changed, however, when he posted a link promoting his self-funded video, which has an interactive, truly disturbing story line where a "stalker" tracks you on Facebook. Even though I was in Budapest, I saw Jason's status update, and a friend in Canada and one in California concurrently sent me links to the video. In less than a week, 7 million people viewed the spot. A year later, the spot has more than 13 million likes on Facebook and has been reviewed in press around the globe. The keys to the success of the video are the spot-on acting and the fact that the video integrates viewers' Facebook photos and location information into an eerie short film. As a result, viewers see a personalized video with photos they had posted on content pulled from their Facebook pages. Because of the individualized story line, many viewers posted YouTube videos of their viewings, many tweeted and shared the piece, and the video went viral around the globe.

But what does this have to do with networking? Having a producer mind-set (chapter 10) and demonstrating your talents via content, presentations, or contests can spark new conversations, relationships, and revenue opportunities. In some cases, it can reverse the direction of networking from proactive to reactive. For example, imagine you're a human magnet, attracting all of your desired contacts. Your phone is ringing, your email box is full of opportunities, and your calendar is blocked with productive meetings. That is exactly what happened to Mr. Zada. After his passion project went live, his sweat equity in the interactive video paid off and became a calling card for future projects, thus helping him build contacts in his industry.

He was signed by United Talent Agency (UTA) six weeks after the video went live, and scripts and directing opportunities are still rolling in. "I was shocked by the results; it has opened doors that I never imaged," he said. He went on to direct a similar piece for a well-known television network and added, "One of the most surreal moments was when I was sitting in the office of a very famous movie producer talking about a potential feature project. Memorabilia from his various films were scattered about, and our conversation was very engaged for over ninety minutes. It's been extremely flattering. I quickly had to become a pro and learn how to navigate the industry."

Oddly, since meeting at 35,000 feet, Jason and I had chatted only by phone. We never met in person until I ran into him again at the airport before boarding a Virgin America flight to Los Angeles. He was on his way to the Daytime Emmy Awards, where he later picked up the coveted "New Approaches" award for "Take This Lollipop." Mr. Zada is now working with major Hollywood studios and television networks to bring his unique brand of storytelling to larger audiences.

Find Influencers to Build Reach: Getting Heads into Beds

Finding ways to connect with key influencers offline is also an important aspect of networking. Peter Gamez, the vice president of sales and business development at Joie De Vivre Hospitality, has been building his network by working with key influencers for years. Not surprisingly, I met him through Virgin America.

"If my network is stagnant, I'm stagnant, so I strategically set aside time each week to grow it," he told me. "Who you surround yourself with does somewhat define you and shows what you're able to bring to a company. Over time, my network has blended into my personal life because the relationships are long-lasting and based on mutual interests."

Mr. Gamez has developed a process for refreshing his network of influencers and tapping his network for value. For each property, he considers geography and the characteristics of each hotel and strategically reviews how to position the properties and to whom. For example, Joie de Vivre has a property in Hawaii. Peter checked his network and he was connected to a gentleman from Hawaiian Airlines on LinkedIn. After talking with the contact from the airline, he learned that Hawaiians want their products to reflect the local community and culture of the area. So he shared that insight with his designers and tried to position the property to be more relevant to his local audience.

Mr. Gamez also tries to match the personalities of his salespeople to the characteristics of the hotel properties. For example, a person who loves bands and music works at the company's "rock-and-roll property," and a foodie at its "high-end luxury property" that sits across from a food market. He matches the personality with the task for maximum impact and gives people online tools for maximum reach. He also encourages his team to network based on their passions. "If you love yoga, go have lunch with the owner of the yoga studio down the street or the founder of our company. People can tell if you have a real interest, and that's when strong connections are made," he said.

Although Mr. Gamez's network has grown, he said, "I've had ten to twenty-five of the same core relationships over the years. Often their influence grew, and so did the influence of my company. There are airline and car rental executives, a senior corporate buyer at a Fortune 500 company, and several other folks. The relationships are genuine and mutually beneficial." For example, Mr. Gamez shared that he has a client who produces the California AIDSRide. "I did the ride. Soon I had done it five years in a row, so we sponsored it, and our employees started riding too. At the same time, the number of riders grew from one thousand to three thousand, so they had more buying power and purchased more hotel rooms." Mr. Gamez feels strongly that if you are genuine in a relationship, the return comes back. Today, approximately 70 percent of his business is from existing relationships in his network.

Another way to increase your reach is to look to partnerships and develop programs to extend your message. Tom Stone, the violinist mentioned earlier, and his associates created a program that included a partnership with local San Francisco schools called Call & Response. The musical quartet visits two dozen schools and provides scholarship tickets to students to attend a live performance. I attended a Call & Response concert and was amazed to see an audience that was a mash-up of teenagers, parents, and senior citizens. There was not an empty seat in the house.

The foresight and effort the quartet places on networking and building a younger audience base is truly impressive. Learn to ask this critical question: who will be your network target five or ten years from now? Focus on the present, but think about the future.

Tune-up Tip: Envision your desired network five years from now.

Where do you want to be? What types of people would you like in your network? What can you do now to build your future contacts? How can you help these desired contacts?

Exercise 2: Make a list of potential reach-building partnerships.

Based on your passions and purpose, consider partnerships or alliances that could help you extend your reach and build your network. Remember to think about your Give Give in these scenarios. Samples:

- A gallery owner partners with hotel concierges and the local tourism board.
- A nonprofit executive asks a celebrity or a key influencer to make a PSA or statement on their behalf.
- A start-up founder assembles an advisory board.
- An eco-enthusiast partners with a manufacturer who makes jeans using less water.

Reaching critical mass can be achieved in small steps or big leaps, so it's important to set goals, understand your target, and look for key influencers, partnerships, and programs that can help you extend your reach and build your secondary circles. If you build connections with your passion and purpose in mind, the return of your efforts will be multifold.

Chapter 11: Summary

Step 11: Develop partnerships to extend your reach.

Exercise 1. Identify ways other than blogging to extend your reach.

Tune-up Tip: Consider Change.org and Kickstarter as potential online platforms to spread your ideas or message or to raise funds.

Tune-up Tip: Envision your desired network five years from now.

Exercise 2. Make a list of potential reach-building partnerships.

Top Tips

1. Remember the value of reach versus revenue.
2. Be authentic and passionate.
3. Identify and target key influencers.
4. Combine press and social media efforts for accelerated reach.
5. Consider hosting social media chats and posting videos.
6. Examine the value of partnerships.
7. Remember that great content can open doors and extend your reach.
8. Look for the right community in the right place at the right time.
9. Make your story or message relatable, simple, and clear.
10. Remember that key influences can have tremendous impact.

12

The Ask

Clarifying Requests, Interviewing, and
Making Successful Pitches

Get your foot in the door, secure a meeting, or simply get advice;
the Ask is a skill people hone over time. With the support of
your network, learn to ask for help, move your projects forward,
and live your purpose.

Over the last year, I've thought a lot about exceptional networkers and what makes them such. One night, I decided I needed
to interview former president Bill Clinton, an über-networker
if there ever was one. I reviewed my contacts and found I had a
few contacts who are one degree away from Clinton. It was a big
"ask," but I called one of these friends to see if he would forward
an email to the former president. My friend didn't hesitate but
did say, "Don't get your hopes up." I penned an email with a specific ask and attached a short bio to my note. Within twenty-four
hours, President Clinton's team emailed me that they had received the communication. Within seventy-two hours, I received
a thoughtful decline to the request. My friend texted, "Sorry, I
knew it wouldn't work." But I assured him, "It's not about the
yes or the no, it's about trying, and I appreciate your willingness
to help." In all honesty, the "no" didn't upset me at all. President

Clinton's time is valuable, and he's working on global issues more important than my book. But that didn't stop me from asking, and the possibility of rejection shouldn't stop you either. You should always ask. And ask again. Because some day the answer to your ask will be "yes."

Step 12: Learn to make successful asks.

In this chapter there will be three exercises. In Exercise 1, you will take your list of three people you would like to meet from chapter 6 and contact them in an attempt to secure a meeting or dialogue. In Exercise 2, you will prepare a ten-minute speech and rehearse it in front of a friend.

Although your ask will differ based on your goals and purpose, keep a few strategies in mind that will improve your success rate. First, if your network is based on authentic intentions and shared passions and you live a Give Give Get mentality, making an ask may in fact be viewed as cocreation or collaboration. You also need to work at being a good storyteller while understanding the importance of a talk-to-listen ratio and constructing an effective show-and-tell when possible. Succeeding at the ask requires a blend of courage, passion for your work, preparation, innovation, and resilience. My friend Michael Sucsy has all of those traits.

A Filmmaker Breaks into Hollywood with Preparation and Passion

Half a dozen years ago, the filmmaker Michael Sucsy and I dined at an outdoor café in San Francisco. Mr. Sucsy, who used to date a friend of mine, had studied international relations and law in college but after graduation soon transitioned into the advertising industry. After that, he went back to graduate school, earned a master's degree in film from Art Center College of Design in Los Angeles, and started directing commercials. When we met for lunch, Mr. Sucsy had put his commercial directing career on hold and was couch surfing, doing odd manual labor jobs, and answering phones at a law office to cover the bills so he could focus on making a passion project. He had set his sights on making his first feature film, a reenvisioning of the story behind *Grey Gardens*, a 1975 cult classic documentary by the Maysles brothers about the eccentric relatives of Jacqueline Kennedy Onassis, a mother and daughter named Edith Ewing Bouvier Beale and Edith Bouvier Beale (Big Edie and Little Edie), who lived in the famed East Hampton estate of Grey Gardens and whose descent into poverty and squalor became the stuff of legend. Mr. Sucsy spent every moment of his free time researching the story and writing a script, knowing that one day it would pay off.

Fast-forward to nine years later, and you will never see Mr. Sucsy couch surfing again. Today, he's a Golden Globe—and Emmy Award—winning filmmaker, and his last film, *The Vow*, starring Rachel McAdams and Channing Tatum, grossed more than $196 million worldwide.

Over the phone, Mr. Sucsy shared the secrets of his success, which started with his remake of *Grey Gardens*. "After I saw the documentary, I was mesmerized. I had so many questions, and knew I had to make the film. I started with good old-fashioned research and learned everything I could," he said. He went on to meet the executor and remaining family members of the Bouvier Beale estate and gained their trust by demonstrating his passion and by showing he was going to honor Big and Little Edie and not make fun of them. "Some of the family members had been embarrassed by the documentary; it wasn't that the Edies' choice was to live in filth, their choice was not to leave the house. Big Edie's heart was in that house," he said. His deep respect for the subject matter and the people involved, and how he communicated it to those controlling the estate, created the trust and relationships he needed to get the project off the ground.

After he had the rights to the story, Jessica Lange and Drew Barrymore agreed to play the lead roles in the film. "When I met Jessica, we were both sniffing each other out, but I had created an oversized cocktail [table] book that showed my ideas. It had hand cut pages and hand printed letters. It was beautiful and double-sided and wire-bound with a cloth cover. Not that the package exceeded the contents, but if I had brought four or five pictures of my vision I may not have sold her. I heard she called her agent and said, 'He's a real director' and committed to the project." But he didn't stop to celebrate. "In a film, the line for success is always moving, I was excited and thrilled, but you have to keep moving. It's like 3D Tetris, and it never really stops. You need to keep pushing and get to the next phase." He added, "I didn't think Drew was right for the part, but when I met her she blew me away with her dedication and passion for the character. Hollywood is so fickle, I didn't want someone falling off the project."

Even with A-list talent, Mr. Sucsy had an uphill battle. He had to secure funding and distribution and learn to collaborate with a cowriter. "HBO ended up taking the project, and they wanted a cowriter to take a pass at the script. I was upset but learned they do this all the time. An agent involved said, 'Do you want a hundred percent of a film that never gets made or fifty percent of one that does?'" He admitted that he ended up learning from the process. "My cowriter taught me a lot about what you don't need to tell in a story; the phrase 'Everything happens for a reason' is not a cliché. You have to trust your gut but learn from situations too." Mr. Sucsy broke into the competitive world of Hollywood with a lot of hard work, passion, and optimism. "People think you need an agent to break in. Agents are like heat-seeking missiles; they go where it's hot, not where it's cold. They take hot and small and make it big. But you have to generate your own heat and do the work. You have to turn off your sensor and believe in yourself. There are a lot of talented people who give up too soon," he added.

Mr. Sucsy's experience shows us that to have a successful ask it's important to be direct, honest, and committed to your own success. Mr. Sucsy didn't wait to be discovered; he created his own vision and was willing to ask for what he wanted and to be flexible when he received valuable guidance in order to achieve his dream.

Tune-up Tip: Remember Give Give Get before the ask.

Before making an ask, consider if you've practiced a Give Give Get mentality in the relationship. Don't overask or burden relationships with unrealistic expectations of gets. Please be considerate, kind, and authentic.

Exercise 1: Research and reach out to the three contacts you listed in chapter 6.

Approach them with an ask. Regardless of the outcome, there is an opportunity for growth or learning there.

1. Research and find their contact information.
2. Write a letter.
3. Send an email.
4. Use social media to connect.
5. Try to secure a meeting.
6. Be authentic and well prepared.

Martha Stewart and the Fabulous Beekman Boys

Dr. Brent Ridge also learned the art of the ask. In 2004, Dr. Ridge was working at Mount Sinai Hospital in New York City; he was overseeing the development of a center and research facility for the care of aging adults. "The project had been discussed for over a decade when it landed on my desk. The first thing I did was make a list of 'starchitects,' or well-known architects, that might be interested in the project," he said. Dr. Ridge wrote a carefully crafted letter to I. M. Pei, who is often called "the master of modern architecture." Several days later, after Dr. Ridge had seen a patient, his assistant said, "Mr. Pei is on the phone." Dr. Ridge recounted, "Mr. Pei had read the letter and said he would love to take on the project with his son C. C. Pei, who had done work in health care design."

With architects lined up, Dr. Ridge needed to find a benefactor. "I wanted someone who demonstrated the idea of vitality, energy, and aging well, and of course Martha Stewart has always been known for her productivity, so she was at the top of my list," said Dr. Ridge. At the time, Ms. Stewart was on trial for insider trading, for which she would later be convicted and incarcerated at Federal Prison Camp Alderson in West Virginia. "I developed a business plan and charted out why I thought she should be attached to the project. She had grown up with the baby boomers, and they needed a role model. Her efforts would give her credibility in a marketplace that no one owned," he told me. Concurrently, he saw a satire piece that appeared in *New York* magazine with "care package ideas for Martha, her address at Alderson, and her prison number." So he sent his proposal or "care package" to Ms. Stewart. "A couple days later, there was a news report that Martha was receiving thousands of letters, so I found the largest envelope I could with a Mount Sinai logo on it and sent in another copy to increase my chances that she'd see it," he said.

Two months later, Dr. Ridge received an email from Ms. Stewart's assistant saying, "Martha is interested in the project, and she'd like you to meet with her daughter, Alexis, to discuss it." That meeting was a success, and soon he was invited to meet Ms. Stewart at her home in Bedford after she was released from prison. "I walked up to the house and thought there would be an assistant to greet me. The screen door was open, and I hear someone say 'Come in,' so I enter, take off my shoes and I see a silhouette of a person coming toward me. She was so thin I thought it must be Martha's assistant." As it turns out, it was Martha. The two discussed the proposal, and she agreed to fund the project on the spot.

I asked Dr. Ridge how he had closed the deal, and he said, "Anytime you are approaching someone, figure out how you can help him or her. I don't care if you're Mother Teresa or the Dalai Lama; you are always self-interested. In life, you get the things that you need by figuring out how you can advance someone else."

Ms. Stewart donated $5 million and her design expertise to the building that opened in 2007. By that time, Dr. Ridge had taken a position at Ms. Stewart's company and was leading a new division focused on "healthy living, not just good living." But in 2008, things took a dramatic turn for Dr. Ridge and his partner, Josh Kilmer-Purcell, a writer and businessperson. Dr. Ridge and Mr. Kilmer-Purcell both lost their jobs when the financial markets collapsed, just six months after they had closed on a large farmhouse in upstate New York. "By force we had to make the farm sustainable; otherwise we couldn't afford it. We were depressed for a couple of months, as everyone was losing their jobs, but we sat down and figured out our assets. We're creative, we had goats, we had a beautiful farmhouse, and we understood media. We started a blog and then put recipes on the site. Web traffic started to build, and we made our first batch of goat milk soap," said Dr. Ridge. Soon the duo starting selectively pitching their story to contacts in their networks, and articles about their soap appeared in *Vanity Fair*, *DailyCandy*, and *The New York Times*. Ultimately, the pair landed and appeared in a reality show called *The Fabulous Beekman Boys*.

Dr. Ridge noted, "It could have been the case that two city guys—gay guys with the largest house in the community—wouldn't be accepted in a rural area. But we came to the area without a superiority complex and admitted, 'We're idiots at this way of life, how can you help us?'" When Dr. Ridge and his partner started to raise chickens and pigs, they went to their neighbors and asked, "What do we need?" Dr. Ridge added, "Our approach helped us assimilate into the community. We enabled all the experts that were around us to teach us." He and his partner now work with twenty-two local craftspeople in the area and sell products online and through several distribution channels. "Because of our television show and business, we've been able to help many people make a living and have preserved a very American way of making products, and we're very proud of that," he told me. "We even started a Harvest Festival to show how wonderful the farmers, businesses, and craftspeople are in the area. The first year we had eight hundred people show up, the second year we had five thousand people, including Rosie O'Donnell. Last year eight thousand people came, and this year we expect ten thousand guests. The Department of Transportation even puts up a blinking sign that says 'Caution: Harvest Festival.'

"It hasn't always been easy, and we've made a lot of sacrifices, but we're working toward a goal and we can see the positive impact our company has had on the community. Sometimes at a big company you can't see the impact of your decisions, but we see the impact of our decisions every day," concluded Dr. Ridge.

Tune-up Tip: Practice quality over quantity asks.

When making asks, it is important to bring the right ask to the right person at the right time. Dr. Ridge's ask to Ms. Stewart is a perfect example of a high-quality, well-considered, thoughtful ask.

Another important aspect of the ask is learning how to be a good storyteller. Over the years, I've been involved in numerous advertising agency new-business pitches, and I can tell you that as in *Mad Men*, there is a dramatic, nerve-wracking quality to a pitch meeting that captures the dread and the joy of the ask like no other. You have to know your audience, look for insights to help you connect, keep your presentation simple, and be prepared. Never overwhelm people with a PowerPoint presentation full of data unless you are making a financial presentation or have the letters CFO in your title. Several additional speaking tips include:

- Never talk down to your audience.
- Use "we" rather than "I" as much as possible to connect with the audience.
- Don't overcaffeinate yourself or present on an empty stomach.
- Begin or close with a thank-you.
- List three things you'd like the audience to take away pre- or postspeech.
- Be human.

On that last point, I was recently onstage at a conference with approximately six hundred attendees. My presentation was after a team from *Sesame Street* that included the Muppet Grover and before Emeril Lagasse. As if that weren't enough pressure, in the middle of my presentation a track of disco music started to play. I paused; the music stopped and then bellowed up again. Rather than being upset, I smiled, did a little dance move, and said, "I've always wanted to take an improvisation class. Now might be a good time to start." The audience laughed, and thankfully the music dissolved. Be ready for the unexpected, and always try to connect with your audience.

A Politician's Tale: The Magic of Storytelling

One person who has learned to connect with audiences is Lieutenant Governor Gavin Newsom of California. "When I'm relaxed, it makes others relaxed, and I tend to connect. I am also always very, very prepared," he told me. Mr. Newsom's good preparation is due partly to a barrier he has worked to overcome, dyslexia. "I can't read a book or a newspaper without my mind wandering, I have learned to underline everything, take notes, and I make my own CliffsNotes. I have binders of notes on the books I have read. When I do that, I have perfect recall." He added, "Because of dyslexia I had lots of self-esteem issues and felt inadequate, but my mom, who was a waitress, taught me to work fifteen times harder than everyone else, and preparation gives me confidence." He added, "I joke that when I see authors on C-SPAN, I know their books and material better than they do."

The lieutenant governor added that he rarely uses a teleprompter or notes. "It may come off as undisciplined, but it's actually very disciplined. I can watch the room and move from one place to the next, and I only tell stories that are real. And I practice." He told me that he's seen the power of rehearsing: "One time I was in a car with Robin Williams and his manager.

It was the night before a big Clinton-Gore event. We went to this club, and Robin surprised everyone and practiced a routine. Afterwards, he shared with me what he thought worked and what didn't. The next night he gave his big presentation and nailed it. You have to do a deep dive to see what connects." He added that he presents his own work and not the ideas of others, so he is authentic. "Most of the time, people don't remember what you say; they remember how you make them feel." For example, a reliable way to connect on an emotional level is to look for stories and examples that help demonstrate and tell your point. Don't tell a story solely with facts and figures, and know your presentation well enough to make it without visuals if needed.

Still curious about President Clinton and knowing that the lieutenant governor had met him, I asked him his opinion about President Clinton's mesmerizing appeal. "He is the master; he has this way of moving slightly into your personal space, into the gray zone. He gets in, but not too far; it's his magic. It's not just about what he's saying or the look in his eyes, it's about how he does it."

Peter Ragone, an entrepreneur and adviser who worked with former president Clinton, observed, "Bill Clinton is one of the smartest people I've ever met. No, actually Hillary is the smartest person. Period." He smiled. "The Clintons are the best communicators I've ever seen. They are proactive with messaging and don't wait for a story to happen. They're also prepared." Peter shared that most of what he learned from the Clintons came from his observations of how they interacted with others. "I wasn't the most important person in the room, but I saw amazing things. First off, President Clinton is the best storyteller I've ever met." He mentioned a memory of when the Clinton entourage visited a Sheraton Hotel, on Seventh Avenue in New York City for a presentation. "President Clinton walked in, and a man working in the kitchen approached him and shared that they had met several years prior. He thanked Bill for telling him to send his son to college," said Mr. Ragone. "President Clinton remembered him and minutes later went onstage and wove the story into a speech about the importance of education. The entire room was silent. It was incredible." Even if you're not onstage or in politics, honing your storytelling skills, being passionate, being prepared, and connecting with emotional stories and insights will make your asks more effective and memorable. The brilliant thing about President Clinton's tactic was three-pronged: it acknowledged a person, honored his achievement, and told the story at the perfect moment to connect with others. President Clinton also wasn't afraid to alter his speech to take advantage of an opportunity to make an emotional connection.

Tune-up Tip: Watch three to five TED videos at www.ted .com/talks to see great storytelling in action.

Which talks leave an impression on you? Are you moved by the data or the stories? What lessons can you learn to improve your "ask" or story?

Exercise 2: Prepare a ten-minute speech, without visuals, on one of your passions or your purpose and present it to a friend or family member.

Have fun, focus on details, and think about what works and what doesn't. A week later, try the same exercise again.

In job search, the art of the ask in getting an interview is particularly important. You must strike a balance between showing the employer your well-informed enthusiasm for the opportunity offered without ever giving off the scent of desperation. Smart networkers know how to turn their application into an audition, take advantage of personal encounters, and be lovably persistent. In 2007, when a recruiter called me about my future position at Virgin America, I never thought I would get the job. I had never been a "client," and all of my work experience had been agency- or consultant-based. I read the job description, and the words "start-up," "entrepreneurial," and "Sir Richard Branson" stood out. Why not go for it? So I sent in a résumé, did a lot of research (and I mean a *lot*), and secured an interview. My interviews started about a month after the airline went "wheels up," or operated its first flight. At the time, there was no head of marketing, and several employees were covering marketing responsibilities.

I was hired because of my background and because I was extremely well prepared and vocal about my opinions. In preparation, I had read every article, post, and blog on Virgin America and many on Sir Richard and other companies in his portfolio. I remember reciting a phrase in one interview that was buried deep in the company website, and the interviewer smiled and looked surprised at the depth of my knowledge of the details of the company and its work. After the interviews, I sent follow-up notes and offered my point of view on the airline's existing creative and media plans. I flew the airline to Los Angeles and emailed some ideas regarding airport signage to an interviewer. Much to my surprise, shortly thereafter I was offered the position, and my time at Virgin America transformed my career, my network, and my résumé.

Another person who received a lot of emails from a job seeker was Joel Hyatt, the CEO and a cofounder of Current TV. He shared the story of how Robin Sloan, a strategist and early hire at the network, had secured his position. "Robin was living in Florida, and he read an article about Al [Gore] and me starting a new media company. He sent me an email saying he wanted to work for us," said Hyatt. "And then he sent me another email, and another and another, each with an idea for the company, again saying he wanted to work for us." Mr. Sloan didn't give up, and, according to Hyatt, "he sent thirty ideas over the course of a month, and many of them were very solid. Then he shared that he was taking a road trip across the country." Hyatt offered to buy him lunch if he made it to San Francisco, and they ended up dining at a restaurant named Paragon near the ballpark when Sloan rolled into town. "We met, and I asked him what he was doing in California. Much to my surprise, he tells me he's here to work for me. Then he adds he'll work for free if he has to. To top it off he was sleeping on a friend's couch in Sacramento and was willing to commute to San Francisco. So I hired him." Mr. Sloan successfully secured his position because he was persistent, and his substantive ideas demonstrated that he had a deep understanding of and passion for the company. He worked for Current TV for several years before leaving for Twitter and is now an author and self-described media inventor.

To hear Mr. Sloan's version of the story, I tracked him down on Twitter, and he told me, "In 2003, I started hearing rumors that Al Gore and his partner, Joel Hyatt, were on the hunt for cable television carriage. Like smoke signals, every six weeks or so I'd hear a rumor about their effort. I had a disdain for the traditional networks, they sounded like old battleships that moved slowly, so I decided I was bound for greener pastures, and I obsessively started tracking this weird television network."

In August 2004, Mr. Sloan tracked down a Stanford University faculty email address for Mr. Hyatt. "I decided to take a road trip to Michigan to see family, and then I was going to turn left and head to California. I didn't send a résumé because I didn't want Joel to think I was a weird kid from Florida stalking him.

So I sent him an idea a day." Part of Mr. Sloan's first idea to Mr. Hyatt is below:

August 1. Plan for the age of online advertising.

The Internet's share of advertising is growing faster than any other medium's. Overtaking magazines, and then newspapers, and then finally TV is not a question of "if" but a question of "when."

Mr. Sloan crossed the country and sent ideas from Wi-Fi-enabled rest stops. "In Kansas, I had to batch several ideas together because it was a long drive with limited Wi-Fi. It was a strange month, driving and thinking, but I was cautiously optimistic." When he made it to California, he crashed with a friend and sent the following idea in his last email: "August 31. Hire me!"

Ultimately, Mr. Hyatt offered Mr. Sloan a job. "We used to laugh about the story, and Joel would introduce me as his cyberstalker. The idea for the network was so compelling, it pulled me across the country," said Mr. Sloan.

Learn to Ask Big, Without Fear

Michel Daniel, a sales executive, also talked about the importance of setting the bar high and making big asks. I met Ms. Daniel when she convinced me to put Le Tourment Vert absinthe, a notoriously strong spirit, on Virgin America planes. I'll never forget the energy in her voice when she pitched the idea. She arrived at our office with the owner of the company and had a presentation filled with creative ideas tailored to the airline.

She closed the deal, and we became friends. Later, Ms. Daniel shared that early in her career she had learned to ask big and without fear: "I was hired to sell Margarita Ice, and the owner gave me a skimpy outfit with hot pants and a cropped top. He wanted me to pour samples. I explained I wanted to go after national accounts and wasn't interested in sampling or the outfit," she said. Soon, she talked her way into a meeting with a buyer at Walmart. "I only got five minutes, so I asked for every store in the United States, and they laughed. But they did give me Texas. I was bold, and landing a major chain changed my career." She added, "If I'm excited about something, I lose my inhibitions and I have no fear, I will always try to close the sale." So don't be afraid to ask big, as you may get something of real value.

Ms. Daniel has now moved to Texas with her fiancé and is considering new opportunities. She spends her day researching products and opportunities. "I'm like a caged racehorse ready to get behind something new. Right now I'm researching farm-raised white sturgeon caviar," she said. While interviewing, she reads everything she can, and she visits restaurants and asks about the product. "If I'm going to sell it, I need to love it. I'm intrigued with the product and am also impressed that the owner of the company gets into the tanks with the fish to extract the eggs by cesarean section. That's passion. He's not in the business because of the glamorous product; he loves the fish and the science behind the product." It's easy to see that Ms. Daniel isn't afraid to ask big, and she knows how to close a sale.

Larry Baer, the CEO of the San Francisco Giants, agrees. "The one principle that I always tell my kids, and anyone who will listen, is to never be afraid to put yourself out there. Don't let anybody dissuade you from your dreams or tell you something can't happen." Mr. Baer shared a story that reflects his ideals. In 1978, he was working as a volunteer at a radio station at the University of California, Berkeley. At the time, he was a junior studying political science. One day, he picked up the phone and called

Charlie O. Finley, the eccentric owner of the Oakland Athletics Major League Baseball team. He said that the word on the street was that Finley was thinking about selling the team and things were "touch and go." The call went like this: "Mr. Finley, this is Larry Baer, and our station would like to broadcast your games. Finley responded, 'Bullshit walks and money talks, how much you going to pay me?' I explained we're a noncommercial station, like NPR, and we can't pay. It'd be like community service." After a bit of back-and-forth, Finley exclaimed, "You've got to be kidding me!" When he learned that Mr. Baer and a fellow student would be the broadcasters, he was so impressed with the duo that he finally gave them a go: "Send me a dollar to make it a legal contract."

Baer hung up the phone, and soon after there was an "avalanche of interest" in the deal. A story ran in the *Chicago Tribune*, and Mr. Baer was a step closer to realizing his dream of working in baseball. He continued, "The point is, I'm sure lots of people would have said, 'Don't waste your time, you'll never get a deal.' But we did. Don't be afraid to follow your dreams. You have to have chutzpah and follow what you love."

It's also important to remember that jobs, funding, or asks can happen anywhere and at anytime. Rachel Masters, now of Red Magnet Media, was offered a job after she helped someone pick up the contents of her purse, which had spilled. "In the late nineties, I heard the most inspiring speaker. Her name was Jeanne Sullivan from StarVest Partners, a venture firm," she said. Rachel could not reach Sullivan immediately after the speech, as a crowd of people had gathered around her. Randomly, she ran into Jeanne in the restroom just as her purse spilled. "Her whole handbag dumped. Oddly, it happened again in another room. So I asked her if she needed help getting organized." Jeanne handed Rachel her card, one thing led to another, and Rachel ended up being hired at StarVest, where she worked her way up from assistant to associate.

Rachel's story demonstrates that being open to serendipitous connecting can have big results. Another key to success in starting successful relationships and asks, both business and personal, is to learn how to listen.

Finding a Balanced Talk-to-Listen Ratio

Dick Costolo, the CEO of Twitter, shared that he learned the power of listening early in his career when he went to Chicago and took improvisation classes with the Second City comedy troupe. "In improv you are making up reality from moment to moment, and if you have a preconceived notion of what you're going to do, you could miss something and break the reality of the scene." He added, "listening is an invaluable skill for a CEO. If you can't listen you can't communicate, and you're not going to hear what people think is important." He said that listening helps him get up to speed quickly and that "you can learn more from listening than you can from a Wikipedia bio."

Matthew Hinde, the executive recruiter, brought up the importance of what I call the "talk-to-listen ratio." He said, "I know if a meeting went well if it was a fifty-fifty conversation. A lot of people forget to listen or ask questions, and they only talk about themselves. You'll never land the job if a conversation is one-sided." This rule applies to both interviews and social conversations. However, in interviews it's often best to let the interviewee set the stage and tone of the meeting. If you find yourself in a moment of dead air, don't panic; listen, take a breath, make eye contact, and add a question or comment to the dialogue if needed.

Another part of a successful ask is preparation and research.

To do that, you have to know what you don't know. When the Reum brothers were starting their liquor company, VeeV Spirits, they often tried to appeal to people by asking for advice in areas where they were weak. "For some, I think the desire to help is just under the surface," said Mr. Reum. For example, the brothers found a contact who had extensive experience working in distribution for an international spirits company. They networked and learned from the contact, and he ultimately became part of their team. Mr. Reum added that regardless of what they didn't know, they always did as much homework on the topic as possible. "Today, all the information we need is at our fingertips," he said. So knowing what you don't know is critical, but that doesn't mean being unprepared.

Lynn Hirshfield, a vice president at Participant Media, told me, "One day a college student asked for a call, and all she had to say was 'How can I get into green fashion in NYC?'" Ms. Hirshfield cut the call short, as she quickly realized that the student was unprepared and had no idea she wasn't in the fashion business or living in Manhattan.

Demonstrate Results: Share Your Vision

Another key to a successful ask is an effective show-and-tell. I met Michele Sharkey through a man who was sitting next to me at a men's volleyball tournament. Soon after the match, Virgin America donated tickets to her nonprofit so she could take a group of underserved youths to Washington, D.C., for an educational trip.

Michele Sharkey is the executive director of the 49ers Academy, a nonprofit that works to keep kids from a low-income, underserved area in East Palo Alto, California, in school. "Either you believe in what we're doing or you don't; this is my calling, I eat, sleep, and drink this. I don't ask for money, I just tell donors and potential partners about our program, and I bring them to meet the kids," she explained. "Once they understand how we're impacting lives, people want to get on board and help."

For example, Ms. Sharkey now has two employees who used to be students in the program. "Miriam and her sister Elisabeth moved here from Mexico when they were young. They lived in the worst part of town, where there is a lot of crime and people breaking into apartments. We mentored both of the girls through high school and college. Miriam now shares her story with donors. It's powerful when donors see the faces of the people they are helping," said Ms. Sharkey. She added that she surrounds herself with people who think the way she does. "When I started this program fifteen years ago, it was very grassroots. Most of the people who pitched in were my friends. Over time, they've become the leaders of the business world, and we've all helped this program grow together. Most of the donors believed in me as a friend first, and then they stayed involved because of their passion for the project."

Ms. Sharkey feels that the key to strong relationships is being completely transparent and to not play games. "I always put the kids first," she said. She also has two daughters of her own. "My kids are getting it now; they know that Mommy helps people, and I've taught them every kid is the same. They may be poor or not have much money, but that doesn't mean anything. I show my girls videos on the program and bring them to community service days. It's important for them to see that not every mom just drives a Mercedes, drinks Starbucks, and wears Lululemon. That's not what life is about."

Exercise 3: Consider ways to demonstrate or tell your story or purpose.

Are there authentic and interesting ways you can demonstrate your purpose or share your ask? Questions to ask:

- Do I have prior results that I can share or demonstrate?
- Do I have images or video that convey the story?
- Do I have any consumer testimonials or endorsements?
- What details can I share that will bring the idea to life?
- How does my idea or purpose impact the five senses? Are those details appropriate or interesting?
- Will my audience relate to or understand the idea or purpose?

Push the Ask to Strengthen Relationships: The Power of Innnovation

Jesse McMillin, the design director at Virgin America, had another tip on the ask: "If you innovate you create stronger connections." He commented, "Every project and every person provides a chance to learn something new or an opportunity to do something differently." He has been known to innovate at every touch point and is responsible for shaping everything from the pink headsets on the plane and in-flight uniforms to directing the look of company billboards, commercials, and photo shoots.

Mr. McMillin shared the process he went through to design new plastic cups, with faceted sides like a diamond, for the airline. "The in-flight team wanted a new vendor so they could get the unit cost down on the cups. I asked what the boundaries were on the project, and they said none." He called the manufacturer and found that the raw material costs were the same regardless of the cup shape and all they needed was a mold. He started sketching designs and then recalled a conversation that he had had with an architect at a dinner party. "His friend was a medical device maker using 3D printers to make prototypes. So I called and asked for an introduction and ended up collaborating with his connection. He gave us a great deal because we knew a person in common. And we made a cup like no one else," said Jesse. He added, "The cup manufacturer was excited, too, as they had not been pushed that way before and usually people just ask to 'throw a logo on it.'" Mr. McMillin is successful with his asks because he "tries to make a project exciting for everyone; that's why I can pull in favors. I let people bring their ideas to the table, we have fun, and I'm always open."

As demonstrated by the above stories, amazing experiences unfold when you actively take charge of your journey. Learn to tell your story, ask for support, look for insights from others, and remember that often magic doesn't happen overnight. "Don't leave before the miracle" is a phrase to remember as you focus on turning your passions and purpose into reality.

Chapter 12: Summary

Step 12: Learn to make successful asks.

Tune-up Tip: Remember Give Give Get before the ask.

Exercise 1. Research and reach out to the three contacts you listed in chapter 6.

Tune-up Tip: Practice quality over quantity asks.

Tune-up Tip: Watch three to five TED videos at www.ted.com/talks to see great storytelling in action.

Exercise 2. Prepare a ten-minute speech, without visuals, on one of your passions or your purpose and present it to a friend or family member.

Exercise 3. Consider ways to demonstrate or tell your story or purpose.

Top Tips

1. Don't be afraid to ask.
2. Practice speeches and storytelling often.
3. Develop memorable ways to deliver your pitch or story.
4. Innovate to build stronger relationships.
5. Realize that you can find job leads anywhere and anytime.

13

Head, Heart, or Wallet?

Understanding and Nurturing Your Path
to Happiness and Success

This chapter summarizes the lasting benefits of my networking strategies for your worth and wealth—in terms of happiness, fulfillment, and success. I'd love to hear about your success stories; write me at info@portergale.com, send me a tweet at @portergale, or join me on Facebook at my fan page.

When you remove the barriers that are holding you back and engage in life, transformation happens. The relationships and connections true networking yields will lead to new experiences, often new career opportunities, and new learning and ultimately help you find a greater sense of joy and add to your true net worth. I encourage you to share your stories and purpose and go for your dreams. Don't be afraid to connect or to ask for incredible things, and always raise your bar higher.

Over time, I've learned that many of us face the same concerns, questions, and hurdles when it comes to networking and moving forward, regardless of our employment status, age, or location. I hope the stories, ideas, and tools in *Your Network Is Your Net Worth* have inspired you to remove any barriers that are standing in your way and will help you turn hurdles into opportunities. If you follow the steps in this book you will unlock the hidden power of connections to achieve greater wealth, success, and happiness. Before you close this book, there is one final exercise to complete.

Step 13: Decide what brings you happiness and success: head, heart, or wallet? If your network is your net worth, what role do the people in your core and secondary circles play in your happiness and success? Do the contents in your wallet make you happy? Is happiness and success driven by what you know? Or who you know? Or both?

Exercise 1: Reflect on what brings you happiness and improves the true worth of your journey.

While you're pondering this final question, I will leave you with stories and thoughts on the meaning of happiness from interviewees and people I met during the process of writing this book. Their collective advice mirrors the concepts reviewed in *Your Network Is Your Net Worth:* follow your passions, surround yourself with supportive people, help others, have gratitude, and implement your vision without compromising your values.

Head, Heart, or Wallet?

Emily Olson, a cofounder of the food subscription website Foodzie, thinks that following your curiosity as you network will bring you happiness. "Finding your passion can be overwhelming, so I tell people to explore. Think of it like dating. You don't decide that you're going to get married on a first date—that would be too daunting and cumbersome. Instead, have experiences that bring release and enjoyment so you spark possibilities and open doors."

Emily practices her own philosophy, and that is how she uncovered her interest in food. "At first I wanted to be a food writer, and I found the email address of a food writer on the *Cooking Light* masthead. Her name, remarkably, was Kathy Kitchens. I wrote and asked her how I could get a job like hers, and she wrote back." Emily was hired as a writer at another publication and found she was "horribly inefficient." Soon after, she transitioned to being a buyer for a food chain. "That's when I learned I loved product. And then I met my fiancé and became an accidental entrepreneur. Finding what you love creates an energy that keeps on giving."

Om Malik agreed. "I only have one piece of advice: don't do anything that makes you unhappy. That's it. It's your life. Use your own decision-making ability, and figure out what's right and what's wrong. Make your own mistakes, keep trying, and stay curious."

When talking about the meaning of happiness and what's important, Stef Michaels, @adventuregirl, shared that she had recently lost her mother to a long, painful battle with emphysema. "The only thing that would kill me is being on my deathbed and missing a dream. After helping my mom pass, I see that in the end it's about who you care about and not what you did." Ms. Michaels feels that networking with the courage to follow your passion will bring happiness. It's about getting up every morning knowing that you love what you do. She continued, "If you listen to your inner voice, it won't take you in the wrong direction. If it does, the wrong direction will be a lesson. Don't be afraid. Be fearless. Go out and live it."

Dick Costolo, the CEO of Twitter, had similar advice. "I've always optimized for what I want to do, irrespective from whether it will make me money." He added, "I don't know why some younger people don't do this, live the life they want to lead. The worst is when people don't follow their passions because they fear they won't be successful or won't have money or won't get to marry whom [they] want. You need to do what you want to do."

"Find your passion and you'll find your bliss" were the words of Lieutenant Governor Gavin Newsom. He also added that he feels there is a big distinction between commitment and interest. "A committed person will find a way to get to the gym in the rain, while an interested person will make excuses. Committed people get things done. If you can find passion, it will move you, it will be your breath and your movement, and you won't regret it." He also advised, "Take a job for what you can learn, not for what it will pay you."

The film director Rob Minkoff feels that networking pays off when you follow your heart's desire despite everything. When Mr. Minkoff was almost fifteen, he was asked to babysit for two sisters. "An amazing book called *The Art of Walt Disney* by Christopher Finch was on their coffee table. I was mesmerized. It turned out the book was written by the girls' uncle." When Mr. Minkoff went home, he asked his dad, "Can I please have that book for my next birthday?" His dad agreed and gave it to him when he turned fifteen.

Ultimately, Mr. Minkoff joined Disney at age twenty. "After many years, I was asked to direct *The King of the Jungle*, which became *The Lion King*." After the production, he was called into a meeting; the studio was making a coffee table book called *The Art of the Lion King*. "I couldn't believe it. I was sitting at a table with Christopher Finch. He did our book. He looked at me and said, 'Don't you know my nieces?'" Mr. Minkoff's inspiration and career had come full circle. "It's been hard work, but I followed my passion, and I've loved every minute of it."

Jeffrey Halbrecht, the orthopedic surgeon, noted, "There is a piece of old Jewish wisdom from the book *Ethics of the Fathers* that asks the question 'Who is happy?' The answer has always influenced me, and it seems like a universal truth. The answer is that the happy person is 'happy with his portion.' Appreciation and gratitude are the keys to happiness."

Zem Joaquin said that her values as a parent have informed her career and networking ambitions. "The thing I value most is my connection to amazing people and feeling like I'm inspiring others, even in the most minute ways. Someone told me that they want to be a mom like me (the greatest compliment I could receive) because I work hard at what I love but chose a path that allows me to prioritize my kids and have fun. I have hit the jackpot."

The art gallery owner Wendi Norris believes that childhood and family background set us in a particular direction, but that is only the starting point to true wealth. "I grew up with a single mom, and she made little money, so I was fairly self-sufficient from the age of fourteen. My drive to succeed was financial. After many observations, I believe if you are passionate about what you do and smart about how you do it, you will be successful." Ms. Norris tells her children, "Follow your passions, work hard, have faith, and surround yourself with people who do the same; it will be uplifting and contagious, and you will have the support you need when it is most needed."

Many of the people I interviewed for this book agree that doing good is just another kind of wealth that flourishes when you network through your values, collaborative circles, and virtual and daily relationships. Mark Horvath, who is helping to raise awareness of the homeless, said, "I honestly believe that when you find something you love to do and it helps others, you'll find your true calling." The photographer and activist Diana Barnett advised, "Always follow your heart as the wallet comes and goes. Your heart will guide you to make the best and right choices." Her advice to others is "Be kind to your fellow human, stop in your tracks, and check in."

The filmmaker Jason Zada believes the basis of success is values-based teams. Surrounding himself with passionate people has been a key to his happiness and success. "The worst word I can ever hear from someone is 'no' or that it can't be done. There is always a way to get things done. You have to find a place where 'no' doesn't exist in your circles or in your personality." Rachel Masters of Red Magnet Media knows that choosing friends, relationships, and contacts is key. "Do what you love, and don't look back. Take risks, work for free to get in the door, and only keep friends and romantic partners who bring you love, support, energy, and positivity."

Chef Michael Mina focuses on education as a key value to success and true worth. "I have two boys, and I tell them, no matter what your passion is, education is important. You have to build a work ethic. If you put the effort in, you can enjoy things and those butterflies you get in your stomach will go away. When you're prepared, things will be in control, and you'll be better at whatever it is you're doing and you'll have more fun."

Anna Griffin, the founder and editor in chief of *Coco Eco Magazine*, stated, "My head offers ration and logic, but my heart is my passion and purpose and is always authentic. When I follow it, I am always led to exactly where I am supposed to be. Anything you set your mind to can be possible. Don't take no for an answer. When fear knocks at your door say, 'Screw it.' Your life is a gift; use it wisely, live in gratitude, and make it mean something."

Jerry Solon, the actor and entrepreneur, perfectly articulated how a personal mission statement can frame an entire life: "I think your head, heart, and wallet are a three-legged stool. You need to find the balance of all three; sharing equal proportions of weight will create stability. Once you have that, dance on it!" He added, "Listen carefully to your health, and never compromise your heart, mind, or body. When you pay attention to these areas, you'll be a peaceful person on the planet."

Other leaders interviewed for this book share this view of their mission. Michele Sharkey of the 49ers Academy said, "After an emotional week, I helped one of our families that had been evicted find a motel. That night, I flew to Los Angeles, and some friends took me out to dinner in Beverly Hills. I looked around at all these people with money, and everything seemed wrong. I almost had a nervous breakdown, going from one extreme to another. I realized I needed balance. I learned that in addition to taking care of the kids and families, I needed to take care of me. I have worked hard ever since to bring a balance into my life."

Dr. Andy Baldwin added, "When I open my heart as a physician, son, brother, friend, and human being, I feel true happiness."

Brent Freeman, the CEO of Roozt, said, "Money is important, so you have freedom, less stress, and don't have to worry about where to get your next meal. But my formula for happiness has many variables that include family, doing well, leaving a legacy, and being a role model and a global citizen. You also need to be able to look in the mirror and be proud of what you're doing. Don't get caught up in the paper chase; if you strip away material things, what's really important are relationships and family."

Last, with a heavy heart I share that Liz Rowan (Chapter 10) lost her battle with cancer at the age of twenty-one on November 29, 2012. Liz, who was fighting cancer during the writing of this book, said, "I feel like happiness is when you're content with your own self. Lying in bed at the end of each day feeling like each hole in your heart is filled with good and positive things. Even though your judgment can be clouded by the bad, such as losing a loved one or fighting an illness, there is always something good." She added, "Cancer is a big, scary word, but it gave me and my father the chance to have a good relationship. I have two best friends, and can't imagine my life without my twin sister; she is my other person."

With Liz and the above thoughts in mind, I encourage you to think about the value of your connections, your relationships, and your true net worth. What role does your network play in your life? What truly makes you happy? Time and again I've found that the people and relationships in my life have a direct impact on my feelings of happiness, the experiences I have, and the business opportunities that land in my path. I hope the stories and tools in this book help you nurture, build, and grow your network. Remember to look inside first, outside second. Surround yourself with a values-based team, and creatively focus on living your passions and achieving your purpose. If you're facing pivot points, get productive and don't let your social capital lay dormant. Help others, be of service, live each day fully, and, remember, *Your Network Is Your Net Worth*.

Chapter 13: Summary

Step 13: Decide what brings you happiness and success: head, heart, or wallet?

Exercise 1. Reflect on what brings you happiness and improves the true worth of your journey.

Top Tips

1. Be curious and explore to uncover your passion and purpose.
2. Don't do anything that makes you unhappy.
3. Say "Screw it" when fear knocks at your door.
4. Practice self-acceptance.
5. Focus on continual learning.
6. Remember that a strong work ethic pays off.

7. Be kind to and help others as much as possible.
8. Surround yourself with passionate people.
9. Look for experiences that give you a sense of purpose.
10. Don't give up on your dreams.
11. Remember, your network is your net worth—so nurture your relationships and give back.

14

Unlock the Hidden Power of Connections

Review Sample Exercises, Do the Work, and Track Your Progress

Are you ready to take action? Do you want to grow your network for greater wealth, success, and happiness? Do you want to unlock the hidden power of your connections? Hopefully, the pages and stories in *Your Network Is Your Net Worth* have inspired you to take action.

If you are ready to focus on building authentic connections, I encourage you to keep track of your progress in a journal. Do the exercises, review the tune-up tips, and keep the Thirteen Steps to Unlock the Hidden Power of Connections in mind if you are feeling stuck, lonely, or uninspired.

With your Funnel Test as a filter for your actions and activities, make room in your life for connecting and building your network. Remember that technology has reduced the degree of separation between people; you may be one person away from a connection that will change your life or help you find a dream job.

To inspire you to continue your journey, following are three sample profiles. In the following pages you will meet Nick Anthony Schwartz, Jen Dalton, and Becky Reese. Nick, Jen, and

Becky have committed to doing the work and are on the way to unlocking the hidden power of their connections. They have defined their passions and purposes, set goals, and identified ways to build their networks.

I encourage you to keep a journal, do the exercises and live with a producer mind-set. Give back to the greater collective, be authentic, and do not be afraid to go after your dreams. If you have a bad day, use the tools and tips in this book; focus on positive productivity, visit a power pocket, or practice Give Give Get to help reset your thinking.

If you'd like to share your progress, have questions or ideas, please send me a tweet at @portergale or an email at info@portergale.com, or post a message on my Facebook page. Remember *Your Network Is Your Net Worth*. Make an effort to build your social capital and you will be one step closer to unlocking the hidden power of your connections for greater wealth, success, and happiness.

Enjoy.

Profile 1

Name: Nick Anthony Schwartz
Demographics: 26, single with no kids
City: Portland, Oregon
Employment: Social media account executive working on the Nike
                    business
Ultimate dream: Buy a tangerine-colored Lamborghini and build a house
                    on a piece of land in Montana.

Networking Goals
1. Build and define online persona and personal brand.
2. Prepare and plan for career advancement.
3. Look for experiential opportunities that are hands-on, active, or
   have physical demands.

Chapter 1: Find Your Authentic Foundation

Old Conversation
1. I'm not the best student, and I didn't finish college.
2. I'm not sure how my "old life" and passions fit with my career.
3. I don't have time to work out, and my bike was stolen.

New Conversation

1. I'm knowledgeable about social media and often share my learnings with others.

2. If I'm authentic and true to my passions, my true persona will shine through.

3. I'm committed to being fit. I just lost 23 pounds, and working out is part of my lifestyle.

Barrier: I often procrastinate at night for up to two hours, watching YouTube videos of Lamborghini burnouts or other miscellaneous content.

Chapter 2: The Funnel Test

My completed Funnel Test is below.

Nick Anthony Schwartz's Funnel

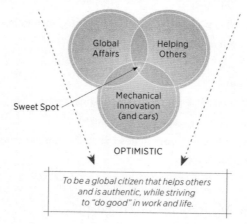

Global Affairs

Helping Others

Sweet Spot

Mechanical Innovation (and cars)

OPTIMISTIC

To be a global citizen that helps others and is authentic, while striving to "do good" in work and life.

Chapter 3: Positive Productivity

I share and collaborate often with my friends and family. Every day, my friends and I encourage each other to succeed in P90X [a DVD-based fitness program].

Tool Tip: I use KakaoTalk to send photos, videos, and SMS texts with my friends on a one-to-one basis or in groups.

Chapter 4: Give Give Get

1. On an annual basis, I give back by building houses in Tijuana, Mexico.
2. On a monthly basis, I offer social media advice to others and share my perspective with people interested in the industry.
3. On a daily basis, I help the interns at work to realize their potential, engage in dialogue with people whom I routinely see in coffee shops and restaurants, and bring optimism to my interactions.

Chapter 5: Shake It Up

I attend a weekly yoga class that I realized was for "yogis in recovery" after I started practicing, but I kept going back because the people are great and I enjoy the teacher.

Chapter 6: Three Degrees of Separation

The three (four) people I'd like to meet are:

1. Valentino Balboni [former chief test driver of Lamborghini]
2. George W. Bush
3. Bill and Melinda Gates

Chapter 7: Build Out Your Core

My core circle includes my parents, my four older siblings, and twelve friends from high school.

Chapter 8: Power Pockets

I work at Nike World Headquarters; it's a power pocket. I'd like to visit more campus-style companies, attend technology events, and believe anyone working backstage at a concert would be great to meet.

Chapter 9: Hub Players

I'm very social and outgoing; I am a hub player.

Chapter 10: Everyone Is a Producer

Most of the content I create is for the brands that I represent. I need to build my online persona and personal brand.

Chapter 11: Reaching Critical Mass

I haven't thought about partners, personal blogging, or extending my reach. This is new to me.

Chapter 12: The Ask

My ask is to move my career up rather than sideways.

Chapter 13: Head, Heart, or Wallet?

I love having a fun, unique car. Just driving my VW bus brings me joy. I'm lucky I have a big family and we all love each other. I'm grateful for my health, being active, having a job, and a beautiful day.

Profile 2

Name: Jen Dalton
Demographics: Divorced, age 41 with no children
City: Ukiah, California
Employment: Self-employed director of Kitchen Table Consulting
Ultimate dream: At eighty, I want to be surrounded by kind, loving people
                 and know I left the world a better place than how I
                 found it.

Networking Goals

1. Plan for the future, increase project flow, and increase my financial revenue streams.
2. Raise my profile on a national or international basis while living in a rural environment.
3. Learn to delegate work and collaborate more with others.
4. Build my community; I just moved to Ukiah from San Francisco.

Chapter 1: Find Your Authentic Foundation

Old Conversation

1. I'm overwhelmed and worry that my interests are too diversified.
2. I haven't accomplished enough in my field to be valued.
3. I'm self-conscious and feel like I'm not making a difference.

New Conversation

1. I'm making an impact and people trust me to get the work done.
2. I have a voice. My opinions matter, and I bring positivity to the table.
3. I'm a trusted partner and a great communicator.

Barrier: **My ambition often overwhelms me and I don't know where to start.**

Chapter 2: The Funnel Test

My completed Funnel Test is below.

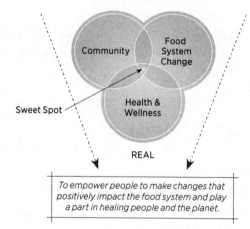

Jen Dalton's Funnel

Community

Food System Change

Health & Wellness

Sweet Spot

REAL

To empower people to make changes that positively impact the food system and play a part in healing people and the planet.

Chapter 3: Positive Productivity

I exercise to gain energy and clarity. I'm part of a community garden, and pulling weeds and growing things gives me inspiration.

Chapter 4: Give Give Get

1. I often teach people how to cook and make healthy choices.
2. I'm mentoring a 7th grader from a lower-income family and hope to inspire her and expose her to cultural activities.
3. I stay present, listen, and avoid gossiping about others.

Chapter 5: Shake It Up

If financially and time appropriate, I'd like to attend events and conferences in my field. This fall I plan to attend Terra Madre, a Slow Food International conference held in Turin, Italy, as a delegate representing Northern California.

Chapter 6: Three Degrees of Separation

The three people I'd like to meet are:

1. Vandana Shiva, founder of Navdanya
2. Bill McKibben [an environmentalist and journalist]
3. Paul Hawken [an environmentalist and author]

Chapter 7: Build Out Your Core

My core circle includes former colleagues from Slow Food Nation, my boyfriend, his sister-in-law, and several friends.

Chapter 8: Power Pockets

I volunteer at local events, I do Pilates daily and have joined a business networking group for women.

Chapter 9: Hub Players

I'm often shy in large groups, but I'm working on this.

Chapter 10: Everyone Is a Producer

I have a website, help edit a national blog, use Twitter once in a while, and cocreated a listserv with professionals in my community.

Chapter 11: Reaching Critical Mass

I don't have much time to write my own articles for a blog or find partners.

Chapter 12: The Ask

I want to add more value to my community, find additional cocreators, and improve my financial revenue streams.

Chapter 13: Head, Heart, or Wallet?

I love exercising and taking care of myself. I'm happy when I'm outside. I feel connected when I'm dancing, kissing, cooking, and spending time with people that I love. I am optimistic about life.

Profile 3

Name:	Becky Reese
Demographics:	Married, age 42 with five children
City:	Traverse City, Michigan
Employment:	Self-employed, launching a fitness clothing line for women sized 10 to 18
Ultimate dream:	To teach others that it doesn't matter what size person you are—what matters is if you're healthy, so you can be around for your kids.

Networking Goals

1. Develop relationships that I can learn from so my business will thrive.
2. Learn to juggle my life as a mother of five and as a business owner.
3. Create stronger relationships in the charitable giving space (e.g., American Heart Association).

Chapter 1: Find Your Authentic Foundation

Old Conversation

1. I'm not happy with my body; I want to hide in a corner.
2. I feel frumpy.

3. I stay at home with my kids, so my worth is "less than" that of others who work in offices.

New Conversation
1. I'm strong and confident and have run more than thirty half marathons.
2. I'm building a business to inspire other women to be healthy and happy.
3. My story inspires others to make positive change.

Barrier: With five kids, sometimes life gets in the way of work. Maintaining a good work/life balance is not always easy. I struggle with feelings of financial insecurity and hate opening the mail. Simple tasks can trigger dread or memories of financial hardship.

Chapter 2: The Funnel Test

Below is my completed Funnel Test.

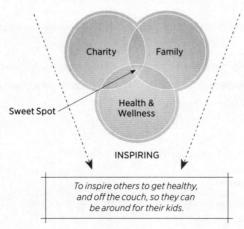

Becky Reese's Funnel

Charity

Family

Sweet Spot

Health & Wellness

INSPIRING

To inspire others to get healthy, and off the couch, so they can be around for their kids.

Chapter 3: Positive Productivity

I work out often, have a trainer, and focus on my health so I can be strong and a good role model for my family.

Chapter 4: Give Give Get

1. I'm giving a percentage of my business profits to the American Heart Association.
2. I teach classes at our church.
3. I started a running club for women sized 10 to 18 that has over 10,000 online members.
4. I am working on my second book so I can share my story with others.

Chapter 5: Shake It Up

I love to travel, and attending running races inspires me.

Chapter 6: Three Degrees of Separation

The three people I'd like to meet are:

1. Anthony Robbins
2. Bobbi Brown
3. George W. Bush

Chapter 7: Build Out Your Core

My core circle includes my husband and my five children. I am the youngest of eight children, and I love having a big family.

Chapter 8: Power Pockets

I've attended several entrepreneurial events hosted by the businesswoman Ali Brown.

Chapter 9: Hub Players

Socializing is sometimes hard for me. I sit in the front row at events and take notes. I don't go out and party, because I want to feel great the next day.

Chapter 10: Everyone Is a Producer

I have a website. I'm working on my second book. I have an email list, and I do some blogging. I'm designing a line of fitness clothing for women sized 10 to 18.

Chapter 11: Reaching Critical Mass

I prefer not to have corporate partners in my business.

Chapter 12: The Ask

I want to show people how to be healthy and happy. My ask to others is that they quit worrying and gossiping about others and start focusing on themselves.

Chapter 13: Head, Heart, or Wallet?

Hands down, the most important thing in life is love. Money doesn't make you happy. There are lots of smart people without love. There is nothing better than the feeling of holding a child and feeling true unconditional love.

Summary: Thirteen Steps to Unlock the Hidden Power of Connections in the Digital Age

Step 1. Assess the barriers that are holding you back.

Step 2. Define your core passions and purpose with the Funnel Test.

Step 3. Create a mind-set of positive productivity.

Step 4. Develop a Give Give Get attitude.

Step 5. Commit to shaking it up.

Step 6. Accelerate your connections with technology.

Step 7. Cultivate relationships that support your purpose.

Step 8. Visit power pockets to accelerate networking.

Step 9. Hone your connecting skills and learn from hub players.

Step 10. Create content, products, or services to share your purpose.

Step 11. Develop partnerships to extend your reach.

Step 12. Learn to make successful asks.

Step 13. Decide what brings you happiness and success: head, heart, or wallet?

Afterword

The irony of this book is that I actually had to live the philosophies in it to make it happen. I lived positive productivity daily, practiced Give Give Get, and had to shake it up often. I leaned on my core circle, asked for advice, and practiced storytelling. I visited power pockets, tapped my hub players for interviews, and made new friends in spontaneous and unexpected ways. I learned about myself and became more confident in the process. I focused on writing the content and pushed aside negative thoughts that bubbled up, such as "Only my mom will read this book" or "You've never written a book, what makes you think you can?" It was not easy sticking to a plan, but I wrote daily, shared rough drafts with friends, and accepted their feedback, knowing that collaboration creates a better output.

I've reconfirmed that when you live based on your passions and purpose, you feel a great sense of happiness and inspiration. I often felt a feeling of elation after interviewing people and was constantly moved by the stories and ideas I heard. By asking people about their ideas and history, you show them that you value them, and strong connections can be formed. While writing this book, I also went on my own journey to advance my networking. Following are some of the behind-the-scenes transformational networking moments and connections that transpired and some of the efforts I'm partaking in to take my networking to the next level.

I'd be honored to hear stories about your networking success, tips you've learned, and how your life has changed or improved because of transformational networking. Please send your stories, ideas, and tips to me at @portergale or info@portergale.com. I'll do my best to respond, and know that your ideas will inspire me. Remember, *Your Network Is Your Net Worth*. If you unlock the hidden power of your connections you will have greater wealth, success, and happiness. Reinvest it. Get out there, connect with other people, live your purpose, and go after your dreams.

Behind the Scenes: My Journey to Advanced Networking

While writing this book, I met some young technology gurus from Canada who had recently moved to the Bay Area and live in a "start-up" mansion, a living/working space where the residents/employees are incubating technology products. The team is behind a social site, and they share my philosophies on connecting, give give get, and being the best you can be. They have a greyhound pup named Indy and a wine cellar that has been converted into a server room, and they have mastered the art of making espresso on a commercial-sized machine that sits in their living room. The walls of their mansion are covered with chalkboard paint and handwritten "I wills," or manifestos and inspirational quotes. "We've even had the UPS guys write a goal on the wall," said Matty Dorey, the founder of the house.

One day Matty said, "We don't know many people. Can you introduce us to some folks?" Together we cohosted a generational mash-up with more than 150 attendees. The team turned the gathering into a connectors' paradise. Lighting was dimmed, several bands played, organic food was served, and tiki torches circled a backyard bonfire. At a check-in table, guests wrote "I will" goals, which became conversation starters, on adhesive-backed name tags. Phrases from "I will go to Israel and float in the Dead Sea" and "I will swim to Alcatraz" to "I will inspire" sparked conversations around the party. At that one event, numerous connections were made.

An art gallery owner made a plan to look at art with a partygoer. A woman who recently sold her magazine company had a follow-up lunch with a potential funder for her new business. A technology executive met the owner of a cable station and had follow-up meetings to discuss a programming idea. A copywriter tried a new musical instrument. A couple flirted and planned a date. A man who owns a bedding company had breakfast with a contact who knows an online sample-sale retailer. A public relations consultant landed a project. A man with a brain injury felt valued. And a girl who was having a birthday—me—had an amazing night. It's true: serendipity and magic happen when you bring people together. That's just one example of the impact of one night of connecting.

I've also taken several new steps to advance my networking. I've joined a mastermind group, which I'll tell you about in a blog or my next book. And I'm starting a salon series at a restaurant and will be hosting monthly gatherings with various groups of friends. As with anything in life, if you want to excel or improve, it takes effort and commitment. I look forward to sharing the stories and insights I glean from these upcoming adventures.

Another example of the impact of connecting is the fact that often the messages and stories shared were exactly those I needed to hear to improve my own journey. I recall seeing true passion in the violinist Tom Stone's eyes when he talked about Beethoven. I was incredibly moved when Amy Rao talked about the generosity her father had exhibited during her childhood. And I had to ask Chef Michael Mina for a tissue when he talked about how his father had supported his dream to be a chef. From one tea with Jack Hidary, several concepts of this book were crafted.

My daughter also informed me, "Mom, you've been a lot more fun lately." Several other people commented, "You seem very inspired these days." When you live based on your authentic intentions, others take notice and it is easier to connect, and a feeling of happiness and fulfillment is the return of your efforts. After my interview with Dick Costolo, he asked, "How are things going post–Virgin America?" I responded, "I'm doing exactly what I should be doing."

The pivot point and my decision to leave my post at Virgin America opened new doors and provided new opportunities. If you're facing a pivot point, I encourage you to live the practices in this book. Define your passions and purpose, and take small steps toward your goals. I live the ideas in this book, and I can tell you that they work.

Last, I've also had quite a few laughs about my intent to interview former president Bill Clinton. I'm not going to let that dream go and hope you'll find an interview or a blurb from him in my next book. Humorously, I did get an email from him when I was penning my final pages of this book: "Meeting You" was the subject line. My heart dropped. For a brief moment, I thought perhaps a friend connected to former president Clinton had pulled a string. At closer look, I discovered that it was a fund-raising email, probably sent to millions of people, from the bulk email address for President Barack Obama. It started, "Friend, I've been in President Obama's shoes before—less than six months to go before an election to let you finish what you started." I laughed. It was a reminder that whatever your dreams or your journey, remember to have fun and don't let a no stop you from connecting, trying, or networking. Be authentic, live your passions, help others, and remember that *Your Network Is Your Net Worth*.

Acknowledgments

This book exists because of the continuous support and inspiration I've received from my network. In fact, I'm confident that it would not have been published if I hadn't taken the steps to remove the barriers in my path and hadn't had the support of my incredible network.

With deep gratitude, I extend my thanks to Tim Ferriss, who held an event where I serendipitously met Stephen Hanselman, my agent, who believed in me, guided me, and helped shape many of the ideas in this book. I would also like to thank Julia Serebrinsky and Herb Schaffner for their brilliant editorial assistance. Sarah Durand, my editor at Atria Books, I'm honored to collaborate with you. To Anice Flesh (my fabulous mom), Gayle Roberts, Guy Kawasaki, Nancy Gale, Edmond Stevens, Stephanie Agresta, Gordon Tucker, Ryan Holiday, Peter Sims, Zem Joaquin, Joel Hyatt, Christy McGill, Chef Michael Mina, Jeremy Mende, Wendi Norris, Patrick O'Hara, Courtney Buechert, Rachel Masters, Peter Ragone, Nick Graham, Jennifer Larson, Gary Vaynerchuk, Stef Michaels, Shira Lazar, Tom Stone, Amy Rao, Jeff Riebe, Christina Grdovic, Jacyln Mullen, Rob Minkoff, Sir Richard Branson, Erik Lammerding, Jeff Slobotski, Lieutenant Governor Gavin Newsom, the ambassador to Hungary Eleni Tsakopoulos Kounalakis, and all the incredible people who shared their stories or read early versions of this book, I am forever grateful and inspired by your efforts.

Most important, this book is dedicated to my amazing daughter, Rylee Eleanor Blum. I love you with all my heart. Remember to live your dreams, keep singing, help others, be creative, and surround yourself with supportive, inspiring friends. You are, and will always be, my greatest gift.

References, Additional Reading, and Twitter Handles

Introduction

Baker, Wayne E. *Networking Smart: How to Build Relationships for Personal and Organizational Success.* New York: McGraw-Hill, 1994.

Christakis, Nicholas A., and James Fowler. *Connected: The Surprising Power of Our Social Networks and How They Shape Our Lives.* New York: Little, Brown, 2009.

———. "Exploring How We Connect, and What It Means." Interview on NPR, September 25, 2009. www.npr.org/templates/story/story.php?storyId=113208990.

Deloitte. "2010 Ethics & Workplace Survey." www.deloitte.com/assets/Dcom-UnitedStates/Local%20Assets/Documents/us_2010_Ethics_and_Workplace_Survey_report_071910.pdf.

Kawasaki, Guy. *Enchantment: The Art of Changing Hearts, Minds, and Actions.* New York: Portfolio/Penguin, 2011.

Putnam, Robert D. "Bowling Alone: America's Declining Social Capital." *Journal of Democracy* 6, no. 1 (January 1995): 65–78. www.saddleback.edu/faculty/agordon/documents/Bowling_Alone.pdf.

Stix, Gary. "Your Brain on *Facebook*: Bigger Social Networks Expand the Size of Neural Networks." *Scientific American*, November 3,

2011. www.scientificamerican.com/article.cfm?id=your-brain-on-facebook.

Twitter handles: Guy Kawasaki @guykawasaki, Porter Gale @portergale.

Chapter 1: Find Your Authentic Foundation

Blodgett, Lynn. *Finding Grace: The Face of America's Homeless*. Mandala Publishing.

Carnegie, Dale. *How to Win Friends and Influence People*. New York: Simon & Schuster, 1999.

Ferriss, Timothy. *The 4-Hour Body: An Uncommon Guide to Rapid Fat-Loss, Incredible Sex, and Becoming Superhuman*. New York: Crown Archetype, 2010.

Lacy, Sarah, and Jessi Hempel. "Valley Boys." *BusinessWeek*, August 13, 2006. www.businessweek.com/stories/2006–08–13/valley-boys.

Pinto, Stefan. *Fat to Fit: 50 Easy Ways to Lose Weight* (e-book). www.stefanpinto.com/buy.

Smith, Bob, and Bill Wilson. *The Big Book of Alcoholics Anonymous*. www.aa.org/bbonline.

Mayo Clinic (www.mayoclinic.com).

Twitter handles: Mark Horvath @hardlynormal, Stefan Pinto @stefanpinto, In True Fashion @intruefashion.

Chapter 2: The Funnel Test

Lewis, Michael. *Moneyball: The Art of Winning an Unfair Game*. New York: W. W. Norton, 2003.

Pinker, Steven. *The Better Angels of Our Nature: Why Violence Has Declined*. New York: Viking, 2011.

Taleb, Nassim Nicholas. *The Black Swan: The Impact of the Highly Improbable*. New York: Random House, 2010.

Sternbergh, Adam. "Billy Beane of 'Moneyball' Has Given Up on His Own Hollywood Ending." *The New York Times*, September 21, 2011. www.nytimes.com/2011/09/25/magazine/for-billy-beane-winning-isnt-everything.html?pagewanted=all.

Pinker, Steven. "A History of Violence: *Edge* Master Class 2011."

September 27, 2011. http://edge.org/conversation/mc2011-history-violence-pinker.
Twitter handles: Chef Michael Mina @chefmichaelmina, Jeff Pulver @jeffpulver.

Chapter 3: Positive Productivity

Branson, Richard. *Screw Business as Usual*. New York: Portfolio/Penguin, 2011.
Ferriss, Timothy. *The 4-Hour Workweek: Escape 9–5, Live Anywhere, and Join the New Rich*. New York: Crown Business, 2009.
Lamott, Anne. *Bird by Bird: Some Instructions on Writing and Life*. New York: Anchor Books, 1995.
Sims, Peter. *Little Bets: How Breakthrough Ideas Emerge from Small Discoveries*. New York: Free Press, 2011.
Twitter handles: Richard Branson @richardbranson, Tim Ferriss @tferriss, Peter Sims @petersims, Tom Fishburne @tomfishburne, Rachel Masters @masters212, Jack Hidary @jackhidary, Susan McPherson @susanmcp1.

Chapter 4: Give Give Get

McNicholas, Kym. "16-Year Old Social Entrepreneur Wins National Competition Vowing to Reduce Waste." *Forbes*, October 7, 2011. www.forbes.com/sites/kymmcnicholas/2011/10/07/16-year-old-social-entrepreneur-wins-national-competition-vowing-to-reduce-world-waste/.
Twitter handles: Rob Minkoff @robminkoff.

Chapter 5: Shake It Up

"Gap Commercial—Khaki Swing." www.youtube.com/watch?v=knW1hGwmEXQ.
Twitter handles: Stef Michaels @adventuregirl.

Chapter 6: Three Degrees of Separation

Haefner, Rosemary. "More Employers Screening Candidates via Social Networking Sites." October 10, 2009. www.careerbuilder.com/Article/CB-1337-Getting-Hired-More-Employers-Screening-Candidates-via-Social-Networking-Sites.

Hoffman, Reid, and Ben Casnocha. *The Start-up of You*. New York: Crown Business, 2012.

Kjaer, Gitte. *Mor på Nettet* (Mom on the Internet). Copenhagen: Lemon Press, 2011.

Perry, Tony. "Marine Who Criticized Obama Will Be Dismissed from the Service." *Los Angeles Times*, April 26, 2012. http://articles.latimes.com/2012/apr/26/local/la-me-marine-discharged-20120426.

Zupek, Rachel. "Social Media Pitfalls." September 6, 2009. www.careerbuilder.com/Article/CB-1265-The-Workplace-Social-Media-Pitfalls.

"Weinergate" is referenced in numerous articles, including Petri, Alexandra. "Weinergate—Anthony Weiner's Twitter Image Problem." *The Washington Post*, May 31, 2011. www.washingtonpost.com/blogs/compost/post/weinergate—anthony-weiners-twitter-image-problem/2011/03/03/AGjSzeFH_blog.html.

Twitter handles: Brady Hahn @bradyhahn, Dr. Andy Baldwin @drandybaldwin, Johnny Jet @johnnyjet.

Chapter 7: Build Out Your Core

Putnam, Robert D. *Bowling Alone: The Collapse and Revival of American Community*. New York: Simon & Schuster, 2000.

Vaynerchuck, Gary. *The Thank You Economy*. New York: Harper Business, 2011.

Blue Star Families (www.bluestarfam.org).

Twitter handles: Nike Running @nikerunning.

Chapter 8: Power Pockets

Belger, Allison. *The Power of Community: CrossFit and the Force of Human Connection*. Victory Belt Publishing, 2012.

Big Omaha (www.bigomaha.com).

Grind (http://grindspaces.com).

TEDx La Jolla (www.tedxlajolla.org).

TedxPresidio (http://tedxpresidio.org/2012).

Silicon Prairie News (www.siliconprairienews.com).

Virtuoso Travel Week (http://virtuosotravelweek.virtuoso.com).

Young Presidents' Organization (www.ypo.org).

Twitter handles: Jeff Slobotski @slobotski, TEDxPresidio @TEDx-Presidio, Big Omaha @Bigomaha, Silicon Prairie News @silicon-prairie.

Chapter 9: Hub Players

National Film Festival for Talented Youth (NFFTY) (www.nffty.org).

Twitter handles: NFFTY @NFFTY, Zem Joaquin @zem, Wendi Norris @wendinorris.

Chapter 10: Everyone Is a Producer

Brafman, Ori and Rom. *Click: The Magic of Instant Connections.* New York: Crown Business, 2011.

Campbell, Joseph, and Bill Moyers. *The Power of Myth.* New York: Broadway Books, 2010.

Driver, Janine. *You Say More Than You Think: The 7-Day Plan for Using the New Body Language to Get What You Want.* New York: Crown, 2010.

Gale, Porter. "Serendipity in the Sky: Conversations with 4C." August 31, 2011. www.huffingtonpost.com/porter-gale/virgin-america_b_943954.html.

LeFevre, Heather. "The Planner Survey 2011." www.slideshare.net/hklefevre/the-planner-survey-2011.

GigaOM (http://gigaom.com).

What's Trending (http://whatstrending.com).

Twitter handles: Shira Lazar @shiralazar, What's Trending @what-strending, Om Malik @om, Heather LeFevre @hklefevre, Brit Morin @brit.

Chapter 11: Reaching Critical Mass

Aaker, Jennifer, and Porter Gale. "Can Social Media Save Amit Gupta?" *Advertising Age*, October 12, 2011. http://adage.com/article/digitalnext/social-media-save-amit-gupta/230365.

Gale, Porter. "How Jason Zada Created Facebook's Scariest Viral Sensation: TakeThisLollipop.com." *Advertising Age*, October 24, 2011. http://adage.com/article/digitalnext/jason-zada-created-facebooks-scariest-viral-sensation/230609.

Holiday, Ryan. *Trust Me, I'm Lying: The Tactics and Confessions of a Media Manipulator.* New York: Portfolio/Penguin, 2012.

Twitter handles: Jessica Northey @jessicanorthey, Amit Gupta @superamit, Dick Costolo @dickc, Jason Zada @jasonzada.

Chapter 12: The Ask

Guber, Peter. *Tell to Win: Connect, Persuade, and Triumph with the Hidden Power of Story.* New York: Crown Business, 2011.

Newsom, Gavin, and Lisa Dickey. *Citizenville: How to Take the Town Square Digital and Reinvent Government.* New York: Penguin, 2013.

Sucsy, Michael. "Inspiration in Squalor: How I 'Rebuilt' *Grey Gardens*." June 18, 2009. www.huffingtonpost.com/michael-sucsy/inspiration-in-squalor-ho_b_217635.html.

Grey Gardens (www.imdb.com/title/tt0073076).

TED Talks (www.ted.com/talks).

The Vow (box office results) (http://boxofficemojo.com/movies/?id=vow.htm).

Twitter handles: Gavin Newsom @gavinnewsom.

Chapter 13: Head, Heart, or Wallet?

Finch, Christopher. *The Art of the Lion King.* New York: Hyperion, 1995.

———. *The Art of Walt Disney: From Mickey Mouse to the Magic Kingdoms and Beyond.* New York: Harry N. Abrams, 2011.

Index